Top Business People Praise *Whack!*

"In our work environment, *A Whack on the Side of the Head* has become synonymous with innovative thinking."
—Herb Dwight,
Chairman and CEO, Spectra-Physics

"Roger shows you how to get creative ideas on purpose. Read his book and have fun practicing."
—Dr. Robert Metcalfe,
inventor of Ethernet, Chairman and CEO of 3COM Corp.

"Roger's book has aroused the dormant creative instincts of my people in all positions: clerks, technicians, programmers, engineers, and managers. I'm especially pleased with the effects it has had on people who felt that their jobs were so codified and routine that there was neither room nor need for creativity."
—Pat McMahon,
Manager of Quality Assurance,
IBM

"*A Whack* shows you how to get your locks off, and that's what it takes to get ideas."
—R. Tod Spieker,
President, Spieker Companies, Inc.

"This book is great at kicking more southerly anatomical regions also! A standing browse through innovative thinking beats sitting any day."
—Dr. Alan Kay,
Chief Scientist, Atari,
Developer of Smalltalk

"I just finished *A Whack*...and wanted to thank you for putting together such a well-developed approach.... My work as a research engineer creates a need for as many 'whacks' as possible....P.S.: I'm circulating your book through our team."
—Mark Taylor,
Atari Corporate Research

"*Whack* is a terrific book.... I am recommending a whack on the side of the head to many people."
—Pierre Bierre,
Clairvoyant Systems

WHACK Wins More Raves!

"A *Whack* is essential reading for anyone who puts a premium on creative thinking."

—Stewart Alsop II,
Editor, *ISO World*

"A *Whack on the Side of the Head* is an agreeable bit of mental exercise that shows that creativity in business is the result of playfulness, good humor, and the ability to leave aside logic, practicality, and conventional wisdom once in a while. It is handsomely designed, cleverly illustrated, and full of entrepreneurial success stories about the brash young innovators of silicon valley."

—*Los Angeles Times*

"A *Whack on the Side of the Head* is a fun, interesting, light, and easy-to-read book about how to bypass some of those mental blocks we all have to creative thinking...it might help you get that million-dollar idea that has eluded you for so long."

—*Info World: The Newsweekly for Microcomputer Users*

"Undoubtedly one of the most stimulating books on innovation and creativity today."

—David Fairies,
Editor, *Concise Book Reviews*

"A book that helps get the mental juices flowing....[C]ontains witty observations...and mind ticklers."

—*Inc.*

"I was introduced to Creative Think on a flight to Los Angeles and read your book *A Whack on the Side of the Head.* Please accept my congratulations: It is *wonderful.* In a society that tries so hard to fit everyone into the same mold, you are a breath of fresh air."

—Adeline J. Hackett, Ph.D.,
Director of Peralta Cancer
Research Institute

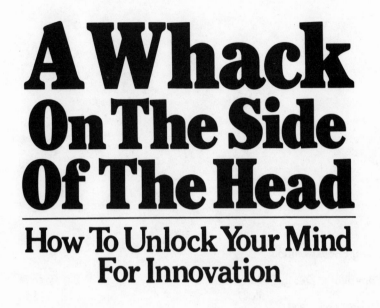

A Whack
On The Side
Of The Head

How To Unlock Your Mind
For Innovation

Roger von Oech, Ph.D.

Foreword by Nolan Bushnell
Illustrated by George Willett

WARNER BOOKS

A Warner Communications Company

Warner Books Edition

Warner Books, Inc., 666 Fifth Avenue, New York, NY 10103

A Warner Communications Company

Printed in the United States of America
First Warner Books Printing: October 1983
10 9 8

Library of Congress Cataloging in Publication Data

Von Oech, Roger.
  A whack on the side of the head.

  Bibliography: p.
  Includes index.
  1. Creative thinking. 2. Success. I. Title.
BF408.V58   1983   153.3'5   83-12489
ISBN 0-446-38635-9 (U.S.A.)
ISBN 0-446-38909-9 (Can.)

To Wendy and Athena

Table of Contents

Foreword by Nolan Bushnell

When Roger asked me to write a foreword for his book, I was delighted. I think everyone needs an occasional whack on the side of the head to stimulate their thinking and this book certainly does do that. It's based on Roger's experiences the past few years helping people in business throughout the country to generate, manage, and apply ideas more effectively. I believe that his ideas will help you unlock your mind for more innovative thinking, and we certainly need a lot more of that.

One of the benefits of writing the foreword is that it entitles me to share a few of my own ideas on the subject. Personally, I believe that innovation is a lot of fun. This is what has motivated me to try the various things I've done. You see, I love to build. When I was a kid, my favorite toy was my erector set. Since then I've gone on to engineering and then to business. I see each of these activities as a subset of the other. The creative aspects of how something is put together whether it's a toy bridge, or an array of integrated circuits, or a new company really excite me. With the toy bridge, you have to balance the pieces to create a sturdy structure. When you're building a new company, you have to create a product that people want, have hiring policies that attract good people, and provide an environment where they can be efficient and innovative.

I've discovered that innovative people share certain characteristics. For one thing, they feel a sense of urgency—a desire to make their ideas happen. And they want to do them now, not next week, not the day after tomorrow, but right now. I like to set difficult deadlines for myself. That's because I believe that the ultimate inspiration is the deadline. Most people allow their jobs to expand to the time that's allotted. I think that one of the things that has made American business successful in meeting deadlines is the "Trade Show" phenomenon. The fact that twice a year, the creative talent in this country is working until midnight to get something ready for the trade shows is very good for the economy. Without this kind of pressure, things would turn to mashed potatoes.

I've also found that innovative people have a passion for what they do. I don't know if this passion is innate or not, but it can be snuffed out in a person. Think about it: how much passion will Johnny exhibit if after every time he runs around the house and displays passion, he gets hit on the head and is told to "Sit down"? You're right, not much. This is one of the things that makes being a parent such a challenge. I see characteristics in my kids that in an adult would be fantastic, and yet occasionally they drive me nuts. Sometimes, I have to catch myself and stop and listen to them. If I just say no, they will probably lose the inventiveness and imagination they will need to be creative when they grow up.

I agree with Roger's premise about "mental locks." Many times our own attitudes prevent us from being creative. While these "mental locks" are appropriate for most of what we do, they get in the way when we are trying to be innovative. I have tried to keep my thinking flexible and free from these fetters. Here are a few thoughts I have on how I keep some of these locks from affecting my thinking.

Mental Lock #3: "Follow The Rules." For years, a standard rule in pinball game design was the 26″ wide playing field. Whenever designers tried to improve the game, they spent their time thinking of adding more bumpers, more flippers, and more targets. The problem was that they confined themselves to too narrow a field, and thus asked the wrong questions. I decided that I could make the game better by changing the width to 30″. At that point, I increased its possibilities and its playability. I learned then not to be afraid to break the rules if it would lead to new ideas.

Mental Lock #9: "Don't Be Foolish." I give myself the license to play the fool. I think that playing the fool allows people not to take themselves too seriously, and when that happens, they loosen up their thinking and come up with more ideas.

Mental Lock #7: "Play Is Frivolous." I've found that a significant proportion of my "big-money" ideas happen when I'm offshore, when I'm out of the routine. That's because I'm away from the phone and my usual surroundings, and free to try different things. When I play, I think I allow a different part of my brain to be activated. For example, I invented the game "Breakout" when I was running my fingers through the sand on the beach. I find that my life oscillates between being a morning person and an evening person. When I'm an evening person, I'm very creative, and when I'm a morning person I get a lot done. But I like to vary it so that I'm not locked into any routine. And I think this is one of the main points in this book.

Mental Lock #6: "To Err Is Wrong." It's the old story of the guy who has a 100% record and does five things right versus the guy who does 100 things but gets only 60% right. If I can keep the mistakes from being dangerous, then I've done 60 right things and the other guy has only done five. If you're not failing occasionally, then you're not reaching out as far as you can. For example, I learned a lot about the restaurant business from the Brewery restaurant in San Jose. This was before Pizza Time Theatre. I lost a half a million dollars on that investment, but I learned all about the importance of location. You can't go to Stanford and get that kind of education.

Mental Lock #10: "I'm Not Creative." When Nietzsche said, "People will lay their freedoms on the doorstep of the Church," he was talking about religion, but he could have just as easily been talking about having the courage to try new things. Most people abandon the responsibility to be innovative, to be creative. They say, "I can't do it." This is crazy. If you really think you can do it, then you'll go out and do it. I know that my self-esteem has been vital to making my ideas happen—I see myself as a doer. I'm sure that other people have had ideas that were similar to mine. The difference is that I have carried mine into action, and they have not.

It's important to assault your assumptions—as Roger puts it, to give yourself "a whack on the side of the head." If you let your routines imprison your thinking, you're not going to come up with many new ideas. If you do 10% of what's recommended in this book, you'll be on your way to being more innovative. Good luck!

Nolan Bushnell, Founder
Atari, Inc.
Chuck E. Cheese's Pizza Time Theatre
Catalyst Technologies

Preface

Welcome to *A Whack on the Side of the Head.* It's a book about the ten mental locks that prevent you from being more innovative—and what you can do to open them. I hope you enjoy reading it.

Many of the ideas presented here come from my experiences as a creative thinking consultant in industry. During the past five years I've had the opportunity to work with many innovative and/or interesting companies including: Amdahl, American Electronics Association, Apple Computer, Applied Materials, ARCO, California CPA Foundation, Chuck E. Cheese's, Colgate-Palmolive, Cutter Labs, DuPont, Federal Reserve Bank, FMC, General Electric, GTE, Getty Oil, Hewlett-Packard, Hughes Aircraft, IBM, ITT, Kaiser, Lockheed, NASA, ROLM, Sears, Tandem Computers, Tektronix, Varian, Wells Fargo Bank, Westinghouse, and Xerox. I have worked with people in marketing, engineering, data processing, finance, research and development, television, and retail, exploring such provocative subjects as:

☞ How can the tax department of a major corporation be motivated to be more aggressive with the Federal government?

☞ What will the "kitchen of the future" look like?

☞ What can be done to increase the efficiency of solar photo-voltaic cells?

☞ What marketing strategy should a pharmaceutical company use to grow 70% in the next two years?

☞ What can the producers of a nightly television show do to come up with ideas?

☞ How can a company which has grown 5,000% in the last five years maintain a "fun and innovative" working environment?

This book contains stories, anecdotes, insights, and ideas that came out of these workshops as well as many of my own thoughts about what can make you more creative.

I'd like to thank the following people who read this book while it was in manuscript form and offered their ideas and suggestions: Doug King, Peter Borden, Doug Modlin, Scott Love, Bob Metcalfe, and Lance Shaw.

I'd also like to thank these people for their help and support during the past few years: Wiley Caldwell, Bill Ghormley, Nick Zirpolo, Don Stoll, Carroll Skow, Jerome Lawrence, Bob Rogers, Jean Caldwell, Ed Hodges, Howard Mikesell, Jack Grimes, Nansey Neiman, Joe Shepela, and Bob Metcalfe.

Many thanks to George Willett for his illustrations.

Most of all, I'd like to thank my wife (and best friend) Wendy for ideas, encouragement, and for bringing up the word-processing system on our computer.

Roger von Oech
Menlo Park, California
1982

Introduction:
Opening Mental Locks

Mental Sex

In the Creative Think seminars I teach, I like to start the participants off with the following exercise. Take a minute to do it.

Exercise:

1. When was the last time you came up with a creative idea?

☐ This morning
☐ Yesterday
☐ Last week
☐ Last month
☐ Last year

2. What was it?

3. What motivates you to be creative?

The answers I get usually run something like this: "I found a way to debug a program"; "I discovered a way to sell a new application to a hard-to-satisfy client"; "I motivated a cynical subordinate"; or, "I decorated the living room around a different color."

Recently, I met a man who told me that he got his last creative idea last year. I thought to myself, "This must have been *some* idea to have overshadowed everything else this year," and asked him what it was. He replied, "I found a quicker way home from work."

I guess this person wasn't very motivated. He seemed to be saying, "Everything is fine," and there's no reason to deviate from what's worked in the past. But he made me think: why be creative?

I can think of two important reasons. The first is change. When new information comes into existence and circumstances change, it's no longer possible to solve today's problems with yesterday's solutions. Over and over again, people are finding out that what worked two years ago won't work next week. This gives them a choice. They can either bemoan the fact that things aren't as easy as they used to be, or they can use their creative abilities to find new answers, new solutions, and new ideas.

A second reason for generating new ideas is that it's a lot of fun. As a matter of fact, I like to think of creative thinking as the "sex of our mental lives." Ideas, like organisms, have a life cycle. They are born, they develop, they reach maturity, and they die. So we need a way to generate new ideas. Creative thinking is that means, and like its biological counterpart, it is also pleasurable.

What Is Creative Thinking?

I once asked Carl Ally (founder of Ally & Gargano, one of the more innovative advertising agencies on Madison Avenue) what "makes the creative person tick." Ally responded, "The creative person wants to be a know-it-all. He wants to know about all kinds of things: ancient history, nineteenth century mathematics, current manufacturing techniques, flower arranging, and hog futures. Because he never knows when these ideas might come together to form a new idea. It may happen six minutes later or six months or six years down the road. But he has faith that it will happen."

I agree whole-heartedly. Knowledge is the stuff from which new ideas are made. Nonetheless, knowledge alone won't make a person creative. I think that we've all known people who knew lots of stuff and nothing creative happened. Their knowledge just sat in their crania because they didn't think about what they knew in any new ways. Thus, the real key to being creative lies in what you do with your knowledge. Creative thinking requires an attitude or outlook which allows you to search for ideas and manipulate your knowledge and experience. With this outlook, you try various approaches, first one, then another, often not getting anywhere. You use crazy, foolish, and impractical ideas as stepping stones to practical new ideas. You break the rules occasionally, and hunt for ideas in unusual outside places. In short, by adopting a creative outlook you open yourself up to both new possibilities and to change.

A good example of a person who did this is Johann Gutenberg. What Gutenberg did was to combine two previously unconnected ideas, the wine press and the coin punch, to create a new idea. The purpose of the coin punch was to leave an image on a small area such as a gold coin. The function of a wine press was, and still is, to apply a force over a large area in order to squeeze the juice out of the grapes. One day Gutenberg, perhaps after he'd drunk a glass of wine or two, playfully asked himself, "What if I took a bunch of these coin punches and put them under the force of the wine press so that they left their images on paper?" The resulting combination was the printing press and movable type.

Another example is Nolan Bushnell. In 1971, Bushnell looked at his television and thought, "I'm not satisfied with just *watching* my TV set. I want to play with it and have it respond to me." Soon after, he created "Pong," the interactive table tennis game which started the video game revolution.

Still another example of a person who did this is Picasso. One day, Picasso went outside his house and found an old bicycle. He looked at it for a little bit, and then took off the seat and the handle bars. He then welded them together to create the head of a bull.

Each of these examples illustrates the power the creative mind has to transform one thing into another. By changing perspective and playing with our knowledge and experience, we can make the ordinary extraordinary and the unusual commonplace. In this way, wine presses squeeze out information, TV sets turn into game machines, and bicycle seats become bull's heads. The Nobel Prize winning physician Albert Szent-Györgyi put it well when he said:

Discovery consists of looking at the same thing as everyone else and thinking something different.

Thus, if you'd like to be more creative, just look at the same thing as everyone else and "think something different."

Mental Locks

Why don't we "think something different" more often? There are two main reasons. The first is that we don't need to be creative for most of what we do. For example, we don't need to be creative when we are driving on the freeway, or riding in an elevator, or waiting in line at a checkout station in a grocery store. To deal with the business of living, we have developed routines which guide us through our day-to-day encounters—everything from doing paperwork to tying our shoes to dealing with telephone solicitors.

For most of our activities, these routines are indispensable. Without them, our lives would be in chaos, and we wouldn't get much accomplished. For example, if you got up this morning and started contemplating the bristles on your toothbrush or questioning the meaning of toast, you probably wouldn't make it to work. Thus, staying on routine thought-paths enables us to do the many things we need to do without having to think about them.

There are times, however, when you need to be creative and generate new ways to accomplish your objectives. When this happens, sometimes your own belief systems can prevent you from doing so. Here we come to the second reason why we don't think something different more often. Most of us have certain attitudes which lock our thinking into the status quo and keep us thinking "more of the same." These attitudes are necessary for most of what we do, but they can get in the way when we're trying to be creative.

I call these attitudes *mental locks.* There are ten mental locks in particular which I have found to be especially hazardous to our thinking. They are listed on the next page.

As you can well imagine, it's difficult to get your creative juices flowing if you're always being practical, following rules, afraid to make mistakes, not looking into outside areas, or under the influence of any of the other mental locks.

1. "The Right Answer."

2. "That's Not Logical."

3. "Follow The Rules."

4. "Be Practical."

5. "Avoid Ambiguity."

6. "To Err Is Wrong."

7. "Play Is Frivolous."

8. "That's Not My Area."

9. "Don't Be Foolish."

10. "I'm Not Creative."

Opening Mental Locks

So, how do we open these mental locks? Let's turn to the following story for a possible answer.

A Zen master invited one of his students over to his house for afternoon tea. They talked for a while, and then the time came for tea. The teacher poured the tea into the student's cup. Even after the cup was full, he continued to pour. The cup overflowed and tea spilled out onto the floor.

Finally, the student said, "Master, you must stop pouring; the tea is overflowing—it's not going into the cup."

The teacher replied, "That's very observant of you. And the same is true with you. If you are to receive any of my teachings, you must first empty out what you have in your mental cup."

Moral: We need the ability to unlearn what we know.

From our examples, we can see that Gutenberg forgot that wine presses only squeeze grapes—"the right answer"; Bushnell forgot that playing games with a TV set was a "foolish" idea; and Picasso broke the "rule" that bicycle seats are for sitting on.

Without the ability to temporarily forget what we know, our minds remain cluttered up with ready-made answers, and we never have an opportunity to ask the questions that lead off the path in new directions. Since the attitudes that create mental locks have all been learned, one key to opening mental locks is to temporarily unlearn them—to empty our mental cup, as it were.

This sounds like a simple technique, but sometimes it is difficult to apply. Often we have integrated these mental locks so well into our thinking and behavior that we are no longer aware that we are being guided by them—they have become second nature. We execute many of our routines without even thinking about them.

So, sometimes we need a little extra assistance to open the mental locks. Let's return to our Zen master once more.

At another lesson the teacher and the student are discussing a problem. Despite lengthy discussion, the student doesn't seem to understand the point the teacher is making. Finally, the teacher picks up a stick and gives him a whack on the side of the head with it. Suddenly, the student begins to grasp the situation and "think something different."

Moral: Sometimes, nothing short of "a whack on the side of the head" can dislodge the assumptions that keep us thinking "more of the same."

Getting Whacked

Like the student, we all need an occasional whack on the side of the head to shake us out of routine patterns, to force us to re-think our problems, and to stimulate us to ask new questions that may lead to other right answers.

"Whacks" come in all shapes, sizes, and colors. They have one thing in common, however. They force you— at least for the moment—to think something different. Sometimes you'll get whacked by a problem or a failure; sometimes it'll be the result of a joke or a paradox; and sometimes it will be a surprise or an unexpected situation that whacks you. Here are some examples:

☞ It could result from getting fired from a job, or failing to obtain a performance raise.

☞ It could come when you're trying to think up a name for a new puppy dog, and your three year old says, "Let's name him 'Four O'Clock.'"

☞ It could come when, after spending two hours trying to solve a problem, you ask a question which is exactly the reverse of the previous approach, and it solves the problem.

☞ It may happen when a cartoonist shows you a picture of a man sitting in his living room under a sign which says, "Watch Your Step," and there are porcupines all over the floor.

☞ It could come when you recognize a relationship between two things you may have thought were unconnected such as a spiral galaxy and a spinning ice skater.

☞ It could be the result of traveling to another country, say England, and being forced to drive on the left hand side of the road.

☞ Sometimes you'll get whacked by a paradoxical statement: "A solved problem is as useful to the human mind as a broken sword on the battlefield."

☞ It could happen when you break your leg and realize how much you took your ambulatory habits for granted.

☞ It might occur when someone focuses your attention on something you usually don't think about such as why many cars have two keys—one for the door and the other for the ignition—and asks you for the rationale.

☞ It might happen when you find out that the "nerd" in your high school class has become a multi-millionaire through speculating in the commodities market.

☞ It could be a question you never thought of such as:

> "If camels are called the 'ships of the desert,' why aren't tugboats the 'camels of the sea?'"

> "If we call oranges 'oranges,' why don't we call bananas 'yellows,' or apples 'reds?'"

☞ Maybe from someone giving you flowers for no reason at all.

☞ It could be a paradox:

> What happens to your lap when you stand up?

☞ Or you could get whacked from walking into a room and discovering that all the furniture has been rearranged.

☞ It could be a letter from your first heartthrob.

☞ It could be a joke:

Q: What is Beethoven doing now?
A: Decomposing.

☞ Or it could come when you see a sunrise after staying up all night.

Thus, those ideas or situations that cause you to get off your routine paths and think something different are whacks to your thinking.

Sometimes getting a whack on the side of the head can be the best thing that could happen to you. It might help you spot a potential problem before it arises; it could help you discover an opportunity that wasn't previously apparent; or, it could help you generate some new ideas.

Thomas Edison serves as a good example for the benefits of getting whacked. As a young man, his primary interest was improving the telegraph. He invented the multiplex telegraph, the ticker tape machine (a variation on the telegraph), and developed other telegraphic innovations. Then, in the early 1870's, the financer Jay Gould bought out the Western Union telegraph system thereby establishing a monopoly over the industry. Edison realized that as long as Gould owned the system, the need to be innovative was reduced. This whacked him out of his telegraphic routine, and forced him to look into other areas for ways in which to use his talent. Within just a few years, he came up with the light bulb, the power plant, the phonograph, the film projector, and many other inventions. He may have discovered these anyway, but Gould's whack was certainly a stimulant in getting him to look for the second right answer.

Summary

We don't need to be creative for most of what we do, but when there is a need to "think something different," our own attitudes can get in the way. I call these attitudes *mental locks.*

Mental locks can be opened in one of two ways. The first technique is to become aware of them, and then to temporarily forget them when you are trying to generate ideas. If that doesn't work, maybe you need a "whack on the side of the head." That should dislodge the presuppositions that hold the locks in place.

For the remainder of the book, we'll examine each of the mental locks and find out what kinds of ideas can be generated by temporarily opening them. We'll also take a look at some techniques to whack our thinking. Along the way, we'll meet some interesting head-whackers: revolutionaries, artists, poets, magicians, hunters, fools, and self-trusting innovators.

Let's get rolling!

1. "The Right Answer."

Exercise. Five figures are shown below. Select the one that is different from all of the others.

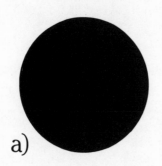

a)

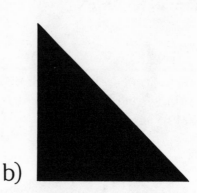

b)

c)

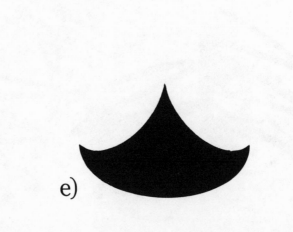

d)

e)

Learning How to Think

Where do you learn how to think? One important source is your formal schooling. From your education you learn what is appropriate and what is not. You learn many of the questions you use to probe your surroundings. You learn where to search for information, which kinds of ideas to pay attention to, and how to think about these ideas. In short, your educational training gives you many of the concepts you use to order and understand the world.

Speaking of education, how did you do on the five-figure exercise on the previous page? If you chose figure B, congratulations! You've picked the right answer. Figure B is the only one that has all straight lines. Give yourself a pat on the back!

Some of you, however, may have chosen figure C, thinking that C is unique because it is the only one which is asymmetrical. And you are also right! C is the right answer. A case can also be made for figure A: it is the only one with no points of discontinuity. Therefore, A is the right answer. What about D? It is the only one that has both a straight line and a curved line. So, D is the right answer too. And E? Among other things, E is the only one which looks like a projection of a non-Euclidean triangle into Euclidean space. It is also the right answer. In other words, they are all right depending on your point of view.

Much of our educational system, however, is geared toward teaching people the *one right answer.* By the time the average person finishes college, he or she will have taken over 2,600 tests, quizzes, and exams—many similar to the one you just took. Thus, the "right answer" approach becomes deeply ingrained in our thinking. This may be fine for some mathematical problems where there is in fact only one right answer. The difficulty is that most of life doesn't present itself in this way. Life is ambiguous; there are many right answers—all depending on what you are looking for. But if you think there is only one right answer, then you will stop looking as soon as you find one.

The Chalk Dot

When I was a sophomore in high school, my English teacher put a small chalk dot like the one below on the blackboard.

He asked the class what it was. A few seconds passed and then someone said, "A chalk dot on the blackboard." The rest of the class seemed relieved that the obvious had been stated, and no one else had anything more to say. "I'm surprised at you," the teacher told the class. "I did the same exercise yesterday with a group of kindergartners and they thought of fifty different things the chalk mark could be: an owl's eye, a cigar butt, the top of a telephone pole, a star, a pebble, a squashed bug, a rotten egg, and so on. They really had their imaginations in high gear."

In the ten year period between kindergarten and high school, not only had we learned how to find the right answer, we had also lost the ability to look for more than one right answer. We had learned how to be specific, but we had lost much of our imaginative power. As noted educator Neil Postman has remarked, "Children enter school as question marks and leave as periods."

The Sufi Judge

These "right answer" examples bring to mind the following Sufi story.

Two men had an argument. To settle the matter, they went to a Sufi judge for arbitration. The plaintiff made his case. He was very eloquent and persuasive in his reasoning. When he finished, the judge nodded in approval and said, "That's right, that's right."

On hearing this, the defendant jumped up and said, "Wait a second, judge, you haven't even heard my side of the case yet." So the judge told the defendant to state his case. And he, too, was very persuasive and eloquent. When he finished, the judge said, "That's right, that's right."

When the clerk of court heard this, he jumped up and said, "Judge, they both can't be right." The judge looked at the clerk of court and said, "That's right, that's right."

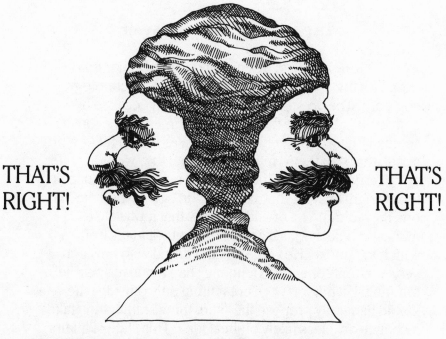

THAT'S RIGHT!   THAT'S RIGHT!

Moral: Truth is all around you; what matters is where you put your focus.

Consequences

The practice of looking for the "one right answer" can have serious consequences on the way we think and confront problems. Most people don't like problems, and when they encounter them, they usually react by taking the first way out they can find. I can't overstate the danger in this. If you have only one idea, you have only one course of action open to you, and this is quite risky in a world where flexibility is a requirement for survival.

An idea is like a musical note. In the same way that a musical note can only be understood in relation to other notes (either as a part of a melody line or a chord), an idea is best understood in the context of other ideas. Thus, if you have only one idea you can't compare it to anything. You don't know its strengths and weaknesses. I believe that the French philosopher Emilè Chartier hit the nail squarely on the head when he said,

Nothing is more dangerous than an idea when it is the only one you have.

For more effective thinking, we need different points of view.

The Second Right Answer

Not long ago I did a series of creative thinking workshops for the executive staff of a large high-technology company. The president had called me in because he was concerned about the thinking environment at the top. It seemed that whenever his subordinates would make a proposal, that's all they'd make—just one; they wouldn't offer any alternative ideas. Since they had been trained to look for the right answer, they usually didn't go beyond the first one they found. The president knew that it was easier to make good decisions if he had a variety of ideas from which to choose. He was also concerned with how conservative this "one-idea" tendency had made his people's thinking. If a person were presenting only one idea, he would generally propose the "sure thing" rather than take a chance on a less likely off-beat idea. This state of affairs created a less than ideal climate for generating innovative ideas.

I told these people that one way to be more creative is to "look for the second right answer." Often, it is the second right answer which, although off-beat or unusual, is exactly what you need to solve a problem in an innovative way.

One technique for finding the second right answer is to change the questions you use to probe a problem. For example, how many times have you heard someone say, "What is the answer?" or "What is the meaning of this?" or "What is the result?" These people are looking for *the* answer, and *the* meaning, and *the* result. If you train yourself to ask, "What are the answers?" and "What are the meanings?" and "What are the results," you will find that people will think a little more deeply and offer more than one idea.

Another technique to find more answers is to change the wording in your questions. Here's an example of how such a strategy can work. Several centuries ago, a curious but deadly plague appeared in a small village in Lithuania. What was curious about this disease was its grip on its victim; as soon as a person contracted it, he would go into a very deep almost deathlike coma. Most individuals would die within twenty-four hours, but occasionally a hardy soul would make it back to the full bloom of health. The problem was that since early eighteenth century medical technology was not very advanced, the unafflicted had quite a difficult time telling whether a victim was dead or alive. This didn't matter too much, though, because most of the people were, in fact, dead.

Then one day it was discovered that someone had been buried alive. This alarmed the townspeople, so they called a town meeting to decide what should be done to prevent such a situation from happening again. After much discussion, most people agreed on the following solution. They decided to put food and water in every casket next to the body. They would even put an air hole up from the casket to the earth's surface. These procedures would be expensive, but they would be more than worthwhile if they would save some people's lives.

Another group came up with a second, less expensive, right answer. They proposed implanting a twelve inch long stake in every coffin lid directly over where the victim's heart would be. Then whatever doubts there were about whether the person was dead or alive would be eliminated as soon as the coffin lid was closed.

What differentiated the two solutions were the questions used to find them. Whereas the first group asked, "What should we do in the event we bury somebody *alive*," the second group wondered, "How can we make sure everyone we bury is *dead*?"

There are many other ways to look for the second right answer—asking what if, playing the fool, reversing the problem, breaking assumed rules, etc. Indeed, that's what much of this book is about. The important thing, however, is to look for the second right answer, because unless you do, you won't find it.

Summary

Much of our educational system has taught us to look for *the one right answer*. This approach is fine for some situations, but many of us have a tendency to stop looking for alternative right answers after the first one has been found. This is unfortunate because often it's the second, or third, or tenth right answer which is what we need to solve a problem in an innovative way.

☐ *TIP #1:* A good way to be more creative is to look for the second right answer. There are many ways to pursue these answers, but the important thing is to do it. Often the really creative idea is just around the corner.

☐ *TIP #2:* The answers you get depend on the questions you ask. Play with your wording to get different answers. One technique is to solicit plural answers. Another is ask questions that whack people's thinking. One woman told me she had a manager who would keep her mind on its toes by asking questions such as, "What are three things you feel totally neutral about?"

2. "That's Not Logical."

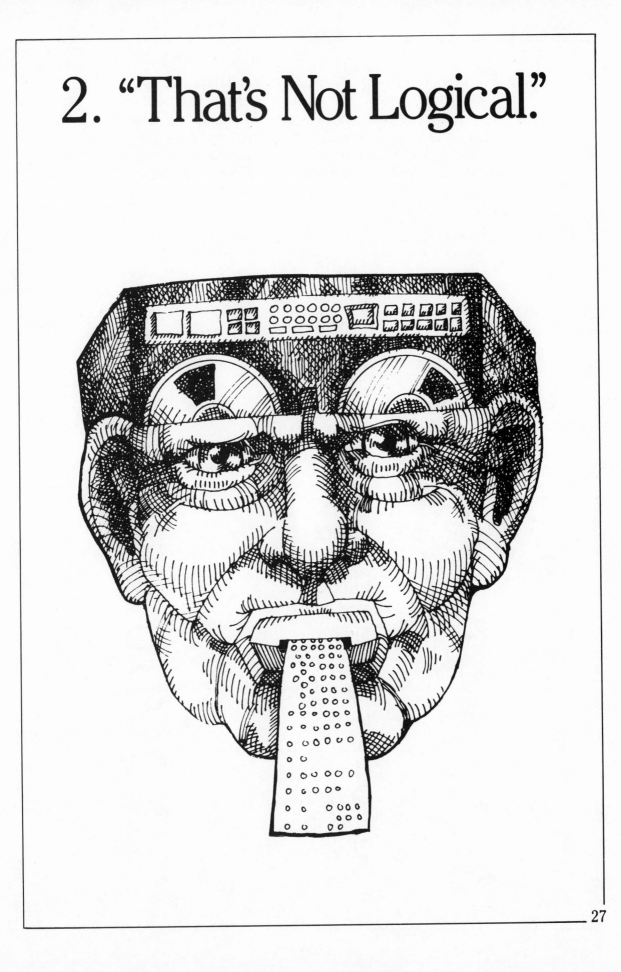

Exercise: Take a blank sheet of paper and draw a vertical
line down the center. On the top left, write the word *soft,*
and on the top right write the word *hard.* Now take a moment
and look at the following concepts. Those you associate
with being soft, put in the soft column. Those you associate
with being hard, put in the hard column. This is a subjective exercise, but you should have a general feeling for soft
and hard things.

Logic
Metaphor
Dream
Reason
Precision
Humor
Consistency
Ambiguity
Play
Work
Exact
Approximate
Direct
Focused
Fantasy
Reality
Paradox
Diffuse
Analysis
Hunch
Generalization
Specifics
Child
Adult

Now take a moment to think about this question: How would you compare the "Hard" list with the "Soft" one? Objective versus subjective? Quantitative versus qualitative? Masculine versus feminine?

Soft and Hard Thinking

At this point, you might be wondering about the purpose of this exercise. Well, the difference between soft and hard helped solve a problem for me. Not long ago, I stayed up late one night and tried to think of all the different types of thinking there are. Here is just a partial list:

Logical thinking	Mythical thinking
Conceptual thinking	Poetic thinking
Analytical thinking	Non-verbal thinking
Speculative thinking	Elliptical thinking
Right brain thinking	Analogical thinking
Critical thinking	Lyrical thinking
Foolish thinking	Practical thinking
Divergent thinking	Germinal thinking
Convergent thinking	Ambiguous thinking
Reflective thinking	Constructive thinking
Visual thinking	Thinking about thinking
Symbolic thinking	Surreal thinking
Propositional thinking	Focused thinking
Digital thinking	Concrete thinking
Metaphorical thinking	Fantasy thinking

I must have thought of close to a hundred different types of thinking. Then I asked myself, "How can I order them? What patterns do they have in common?" I thought about these questions for some time, but came up empty.

I was about to go to bed when I remembered the words of Kenneth Boulding. Boulding is an economist by profession, but more than that, he is a student of life. What Boulding said was this:

There are two kinds of people in this world: those who divide everything into two groups, and those who don't.

At that moment I was feeling like a member of the former group. I thought: "Why not apply this binary insight to the different types of thinking and divide them into two groups." But what would the differentiating factors be? I thought of opposites: good/bad, strong/weak, inside/outside, big/small, masculine/feminine, living/dying, and so on, but none of these expressed what I was looking for. And then it hit me: why not soft and hard?

If you are like a lot of people, your soft and hard lists probably looked something like this:

Soft	Hard
Metaphor	Logic
Dream	Reason
Humor	Precision
Ambiguity	Consistency
Play	Work
Approximate	Exact
Fantasy	Reality
Paradox	Direct
Diffuse	Focused
Hunch	Analysis
Generalization	Specifics
Child	Adult

As you can see, things on the hard side have a definite right and wrong answer; on the soft side, there may be many right answers. On the hard side, things are black and white; on the soft side, there are many shades of gray (to say nothing of orange, purple, and magenta!). A few of you might say that you can pick up the things on the hard side—like a bar of metal; the soft things are a little more difficult to grab onto—like a handful of water.

Soft thinking has many of the characteristics on the soft list: it is metaphorical, approximate, diffuse, humorous, playful, and capable of dealing with contradiction. *Hard thinking,* on the other hand, tends to be more logical, precise, exact, specific, and consistent. We might say that hard thinking is like a spotlight. It is bright, clear, and intense, but the focus is narrow. Soft thinking is like a floodlight. It is more diffuse, not as intense, but covers a wider area.

Soft thinking tries to find similarities and connections among things, while hard thinking focuses on their differences. For example, a soft thinker might say that a cat and a refrigerator have a lot in common, and then proceed to point out their similarities ("they both have a place to put fish"; "they both have tails"; "they both come in a variety of colors"; etc.). The hard thinker would establish the cat and the refrigerator as being members of two different sets.

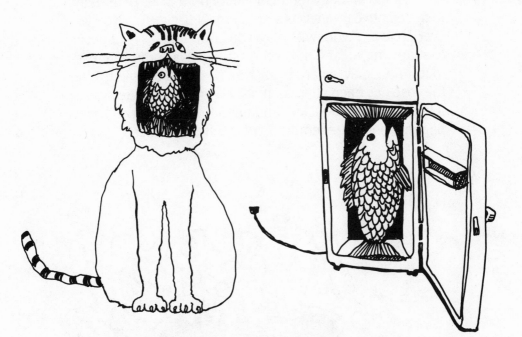

A person using soft thinking might ask a question such as, "What would furniture look like if our knees bent the other way?" The hard thinker would say, "What materials should be used in manufacturing to optimize the rate of return on this new line of chairs?"

The Creative Process

Where do you use soft and hard thinking? To answer this question, we should turn to the creative process. There are two main phases in the development of new ideas: a *germinal* phase and a *practical* one.

In the germinal phase, ideas are generated and manipulated; in the practical phase, they are evaluated and executed. To use a biological metaphor, the germinal phase sprouts the new ideas and the practical phase harvests them.

Both types of thinking play an important role in the creative process, but usually during different phases. Soft thinking is quite effective in the germinal phase when you are searching for new ideas, thinking globally, and manipulating problems. Hard thinking, on the other hand, is best used in the practical phase when you are evaluating ideas, narrowing in on practical solutions, running risk-analyses, and preparing to carry the idea into action.

A good analogy for the need for both types of thinking in the creative process is a potter making a vase. If you've ever done any work with clay, you know that it's a lot easier to shape, mold, and throw the clay if it has some softness to it (brittle clay is hard to shape). By the same token, after the vase has been shaped, it has no practical value unless it has been put into a kiln and fired. Both the soft and the hard elements are required but at different times.

If soft and hard thinking each have their respective strengths, they also have their weaknesses. Thus, it is important to know when each is *not* appropriate. Soft thinking in the practical phase can prevent the execution of an idea; here firmness and directness are preferable to ambiguity and dreams. Conversely, hard thinking in the germinal phase can limit the creative process. Logic and analysis are important tools, but an over-reliance on them—especially early in the creative process—can prematurely narrow your thinking.

That's Not Logical

The first and supreme principle of traditional logic is the law of non-contradiction. Logic can comprehend only those things that have a consistent and non-contradictory nature. This is fine except that most of life is ambiguous; inconsistency and contradiction are the hallmarks of human existence. As a result, the number of things that can be thought about in a logical manner is small, and an overemphasis on the logical method can inhibit the exploring mind.

Some people, however, have little use for soft thinking. Their feeling toward it is *"That's not logical."* When faced with a problem, they immediately bring in their hard thinking strategies. They say, "Let's get down to brass tacks." As Karl Albrecht points out, they never give themselves an opportunity to consider steel tacks, copper tacks, plastic tacks, sailing tacks, income tax, syntax or contacts. If you use a little soft thinking early in the creative process, you may still end up going with the "brass tacks," but at least you will have considered alternatives.

Our educational system does a fairly good job of developing hard thinking skills, but there is not much to develop soft thinking. As a matter of fact, much of our education is geared toward eliminating soft thinking, or at best, teaching us to regard it as an inferior tool. Human intelligence is a complicated phenomenon, and yet almost all of our formal notions of intelligence are based on logic and analysis—look at I.Q. tests, for example. Musical ability, decorating, painting, and cooking seem to have no place in many testmakers' conception of intelligence. As Edward de Bono points out, if someone says he has learned to think, most people assume that he means he has learned to think logically.

The Computer Model of Mind

There is another reason for the "that's not logical" mental lock. As an historian of ideas, I've noticed that the models people use to understand mental processes reflect the technology of their time. For example, in the 17th century, people thought about the mind as though it were a mirror or a lens, and this "mirrors" the advances made then in the fields of optics and lens-making. The Freudian model of mind, developed in the late 19th and early 20th centuries, seems based on the ubiquity of the steam engine locomotive. Ideas and thoughts billow up from the subconscious to the conscious in the same way steam moves from boiler to compression chamber. In the early twentieth century, the mind was viewed by some as a vast telephone switching network with circuits and relays running through the brain.

For the past twenty years, we've had a new model of mind: the computer. This model does a good job of describing certain aspects of our thinking. For example, we have "input" and "output" and "information-processing." There is also "feedback," "programming," and "storage."

This is fine as far as it goes, but some people take this model literally and think that the mind really *is* a computer. As a result, they may dismiss the soft types of thinking as not being "logical." Indeed, I've even seen adherents of this model treat other people like machines. How many times have you heard someone say, "I interface with that person," or "I'm operating in panic mode," or "I need to make an information dump on you"? The best one I heard was by a man describing the different parts of a computer system: "There is hardware, software, firmware, and liveware." Liveware is the people-element of the system.

I believe that the mind is not only a computer that processes information, it's also a museum that stores experiences, a device that encodes holograms, a playground in which to play, a muscle to be strengthened, a compost pile to be turned, a workshop in which to construct thoughts, a debating opponent to be won over, a cat to be stroked, a funhouse to be explored, and forty-three others. There are a lot of right ways to model the mind—all depending on what you think is important.

Roger's Favorite Soft Thinking Tool

To combat the dangers of creative rigor mortis due to excessive hard thinking, I would like to introduce one of my favorite soft thinking tools. I'll introduce it with a quiz. As you do the quiz, think of yourself as a poet. This is a high compliment; our word for poet comes from the Greek word *poietes* which meant not only "poet" but also "creator."

Exercise: What do the following have in common?

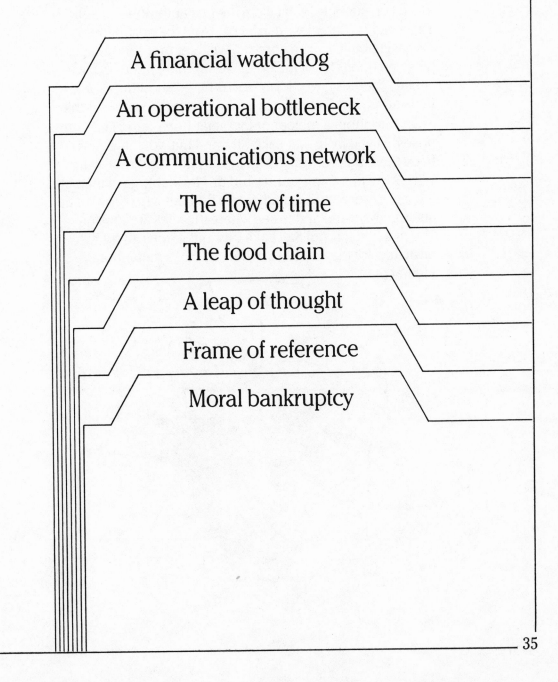

A financial watchdog

An operational bottleneck

A communications network

The flow of time

The food chain

A leap of thought

Frame of reference

Moral bankruptcy

In addition to everything else, they are all metaphors. They all connect two different universes of meaning through some similarity the two share. In doing so, metaphors help us to understand one idea by means of another. For example, we understand the nature of a particular financial function by comparing it to a watchdog (they both protect), the passing of time to a river (flow), and the feeding interrelationship of the animal world to a chain (links).

The key to metaphorical thinking is similarity. In fact, this is how our thinking grows; we understand the unfamiliar by means of the similarities it has with what is familiar to us. For example, what were the first automobiles called? That's right, "horseless carriages." And the first locomotives were called "iron horses." We refer to resemblances between things all of the time. We say that hammers have "heads," tables have "legs," roads have "shoulders," and beds have "feet." It's all very soft, but it *is* the way we think.

How about a metaphor for metaphors? Sure. Let's suppose that you fly to Salt Lake City, and that you have never been there before. You get off the airplane and rent a car. What's the first thing you should do? Probably get a map of the city to see how it is laid out, to find out where the roads and freeways are, and to see where the sites are located. The map itself is not Salt Lake City, but it does give you a basic idea of the structure of the city. So, a metaphor is a mental map.

The Water Model of Finance

Our language is quite metaphorical, so much so that we don't realize it. There are clusters of metaphors that reflect what we think about various activities. One example is the "Game of Life" metaphor. Here, the business community uses sports terminology to describe itself. Everyone is trying to be #1; there are "management teams," "kickoff" meetings, and salesmen with "proven track records." You may also "spar" with your manager, deal with "heavy-weights" and "lightweights"; and, give a "knockout" performance.

My favorite example of this phenomenon is the language used by financial people. Whenever I do any work with bankers or accountants, they talk about what they do as though they were plumbers. And no wonder! They use the "Water Model of Finance" to describe their work.

Flood the Market

Laundered Money

Liquid Assets

Solvency

Deposits

Slush Fund

Pump Money In

Frozen Assets

Float a Loan

Bank

Currency

Take a Bath

Cash Flow

Washed Up

Sinking Fund

Capital Drain

Underwater Pricing

Making The Strange Familiar

Metaphors are quite effective at making complex ideas easier to understand. They can be good tools to use for explaining ideas to people outside your specialty. Some examples:

Dolby Stereo. In the past several years the words "Dolby Stereo" have become familiar to FM radio listeners and movie goers. I'm not an engineer, so I don't understand all of the bits and bytes of the Dolby process, but I heard an engineer recently make the following metaphor for Dolby:

> Dolby is like a sonic laundry. It washes the dirt (or noise) out of the clothes (the signal) without disturbing the clothes (the signal).

I've asked other engineers about this, and they agree that Dolby is a "cleansing" process.

Labor Unions. Philosopher/longshoreman Eric Hoffer once described labor unions in this way:

> Back in the 1930's, the unions were like a 21 year old woman. She was beautiful, had a gorgeous body, a sparkling personality, and she seduced a lot of people into the union movement. That's fine. The problem is that this 21 year old siren is now in her 60's and she's forty pounds overweight, needs a facelift, and has a terrible disposition.

"The difficulty," he adds, "is that she still thinks she is 21."

Cataracts. I once heard an ophthalmologist make the following metaphor for the development and surgical removal of a cataract:

> Remember when it was possible to get a convertible automobile? You'd have it delivered, and the front and side windows would be glass, but the rear window would be plastic. That was okay because you could see through it. After about six months, however, the plastic began to yellow, but you could still see through it. After a year, it became yellower. And

finally, after several years, the window became opaque, and you would have to go back to the dealer to have it replaced. So it is with a cataract.

At first, the eye is fine. Then tissue grows over it. And then when the eye is occluded, it's necessary to have surgical removal of the tissue.

This is probably the reason we no longer have cataract convertibles.

Personal Computers. Steve Jobs, the co-inventor of the Apple computer, compares his product to a bicycle in the following analogy:

> A few years ago, I read a study about the efficiency of locomotion for various species on the earth, including man. The study determined which species was the most efficient, in terms of getting from point A to point B with the least amount of energy exerted. The condor won. Man made a rather unimpressive showing about a third of the way down the list.
>
> But someone there had the insight to test a man riding a bicycle. Man was twice as efficient as the condor! This illustrated man's ability as a tool maker. When he created the bicycle, he created a tool that amplified an inherent ability. That's why I like to compare the personal computer to the bicycle. Our personal computer is a 21st century bicycle if you will, because it is a tool that can amplify a certain part of our inherent intelligence....

In a strict logical sense, a personal computer is *not* a bicycle, and a cataract is *not* the rear window of a convertible. But by using such analogies, we enable ourselves to gain a new perspective on both the unfamiliar and the quite familiar.

The Meaning of Life

As you may have guessed by now, metaphors are one of my passions, and so I hope you'll excuse me for one more metaphorical indulgence.

One question I have is, "What is the meaning of life?" To find the answer, I have asked my workshop participants to make a metaphor for life. Their ideas can be put into two groups: those that deal with food, and those that don't. Here is the meaning of life:

 Life is like a bagel. It's delicious when it's fresh and warm, but often it's just hard. The hole in the middle is its great mystery, and yet it wouldn't be a bagel without it.

 Life is like eating grapefruit. First, you have to break through the skin; then it takes a couple of bites to get used to the taste, and just as you begin to enjoy it, it squirts you in the eye.

 Life is like a banana. You start out green and get soft and mushy with age. Some people want to be one of the bunch while others want to be top banana. You have to take care not to slip on externals. And, finally, you have to strip off the outer coating to get at the meat.

Life is like cooking. It all depends on what you add and how you mix it. Sometimes you follow the recipe and at other times, you're creative.

Life is like a jigsaw puzzle but you don't have the picture on the front of the box to know what it's supposed to look like. Sometimes, you're not even sure if you have all of the pieces.

Life is like an unassembled abacus. It's what you make of it that counts.

 Life is like new product development. Market research is the decision by the parents to have children. Product conceptualization is conception. Development of prototype is birth. Debugging of prototype is learning. Successful sales is working. Product maturation is retirement. And product obsolescence is death.

Life is like a maze in which you try to avoid the exit.

Life is like riding an elevator. It has a lot of ups and downs and someone is always pushing your buttons. Sometimes you get the shaft, but what really bothers you are the jerks.

Life is like a poker game. You deal or are dealt to. It includes skill and luck. You bet, check, bluff, and raise. You learn from those you play with. Sometimes, you win with a pair or lose with a full house. But whatever happens, it's best to keep on shuffling along.

 Life is like a puppy dog always searching for a street full of fire hydrants.

 Life is like a room full of open doors which close as you get older.

What do you think life is like?

Summary

Logic is an important creative thinking tool. Its use is especially appropriate in the practical phase of the creative process when you are evaluating ideas and preparing them for action.

When you're searching for ideas, however, excessive logical thinking can short-circuit your creative process. That's because the germinal phase is governed by a different kind of logic which could be best described as metaphorical, fantastic, diffuse, elliptical, and ambiguous.

☐ *TIP #3:* For more and better ideas, I prescribe a good dose of soft thinking in the germinal phase, and a hearty helping of hard thinking in the practical phase.

☐ *TIP #4:* The metaphor is an excellent tool to help you "think something different." As Ortega y Gasset put it, "The metaphor is probably the most fertile power possessed by man." Think of yourself as a poet, and look for similarities around you. If you have a problem, try making a metaphor for it. That should help to give you a fresh slant on it.

☐ *TIP #5:* Go on metaphor hunts. Pay attention to the metaphors people use to describe what they're doing. For example, have you ever noticed how meteorologists use the "War Model of Weather" to describe their science?

☐ *TIP #6:* Pay attention to the metaphors you use in your own thinking. As glorious a tool as metaphors are, they can easily imprison your thinking if you're not aware how much they're guiding your thoughts.

3. "Follow The Rules."

Patterns: The Rules of the Game

"Order is heav'n's first law."
— Alexander Pope

Let's suppose that you are watching television in your living room with a few friends. Someone walks into the room, and as he does, he trips over a chair and knocks it down. This person then picks the chair up and excuses himself for the commotion he has caused. What's your impression of this person? Be honest. You probably think he's a klutz, right?

Okay, ten minutes later, another person walks into the room, and he too falls over the chair. Twenty minutes later, another person walks into the room, and the whole scene is repeated again. What is your opinion now? Probably that the chair is in the wrong place. Congratulations, you have recognized a pattern! You might even generalize this pattern into a rule such that anybody walking into the room will trip over the chair—unless, of course, the chair is moved.

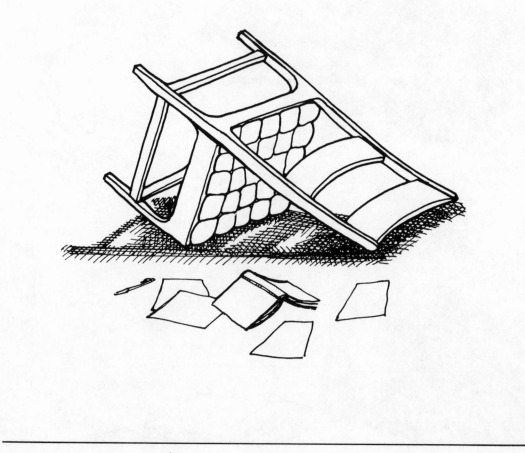

Suppose I gave you the following series of numbers:

$$1, \quad 4, \quad 9, \quad 16, \quad 25, \quad 36, \quad 49$$

More than likely, you would quickly recognize a pattern, namely that each of the numbers is the square of its position in the series. And you might feel so confident in this pattern that you would predict the next number in the series to be 64. Again, you have made a rule based on a pattern you have recognized.

What if you saw this list:

Painted eggs
Fireworks
Champagne
Candy canes
Pranks
John Philip Sousa music
Shamrocks
Jack-o'-lanterns

At first, you probably wouldn't recognize much similarity between painted eggs and fireworks, but after reading through the rest of the list, you would have realized that these things are all associated with American holidays. If we continued this list, you wouldn't be surprised to find egg nog, heart-shaped candy, potato salad, tinsel, the Unknown Soldier, ground hogs, and cherry trees.

With these three examples, we recognize another pattern, namely, that the human mind is very good at recognizing patterns. Indeed, I think much of what is called "intelligence" is our ability to recognize patterns. We recognize sequences (the order in which you put your clothes on), cycles (bird migrations), processes (how to convert flour, eggs, and milk into waffles), tendencies (if I smile at the checkout-counter girl, she'll smile at me), distributions (demographics), shapes (cloud formations), sounds (melodies), movements (traffic flow), cultural rites (courtship patterns), and probabilities (the likelihood of throwing a "seven" at a crap table).

People see patterns everywhere—even when none was intended. A good example of this is the night sky. In figure 1, we see a portion of the spring sky in the northern hemisphere.

1) A Portion of the Spring Sky

Looks like a bunch of stars, right? Well, thousands of years ago, the ancients looked up, emphasized some of the stars, made connections among them, and ignored the remaining stars to come up with the figure of a lion (figure 2)—a celestial Rorschach!

2) The Constellation Leo

Thus, patterns give us power to understand the phenomenal world, and as a consequence, they *rule* our thinking—they become the rules according to which we play the game of life.

Challenging The Rules

"Every act of creation is first of all an act of destruction."

— Picasso

If constructing patterns were all that was necessary for creating new ideas, we'd all be creative geniuses. Creative thinking is not only *constructive,* it's also *destructive.* As we stated in the opening chapter, creative thinking involves playing with what you know, and this may mean breaking out of one pattern in order to create a new one. Thus, an effective creative thinking strategy is to play the revolutionary and challenge the rules. Here's a good example:

In the winter of 333 B.C., the Macedonian general Alexander and his army arrive in the Asian city of Gordium to take up winter quarters. While there, Alexander hears about the legend surrounding the town's famous knot, the "Gordian Knot." A prophecy states that whoever is able to untie this strangely complicated knot will become king of Asia.

This story intrigues Alexander, and he asks to be taken to the knot so that he can attempt to untie it. He studies it for several moments, but after fruitless attempts to find the rope-ends, he is stymied. "How can I unfasten the knot?" he asks himself.

He gets an idea: "I'll just have to make up my own knot-untying rules." So he pulls out his sword and slices the knot in half. Asia is fated to him.

Copernicus broke the rule that the earth stands in the center of the universe. Napoleon broke the rules on the proper way to conduct a military campaign. Beethoven broke the rules on how a symphony should be written. Picasso broke the rule that a bicycle seat is for sitting on while pedaling a bicycle. Think about it: almost every advance in art, science, technology, business, marketing, cooking, medicine, agriculture, and design has occurred when someone challenged the rules and tried another approach.

Such rule-breaking happens in sports as well. Until the 1920's, there were only three competitive swimming strokes—freestyle, backstroke, and breaststroke—and each had specific rules which described how it was to be performed. The rules of breaststroke stated that both arms must be pulled together underwater and then recovered simultaneously back to the start of the pulling position to begin the next stroke. Most people interpreted this arm recovery to mean an *underwater* recovery. In the 1920's, however, someone challenged the rules, and reinterpreted this arm recovery to be an *out-of-the-water* recovery. Since this new "breaststroke" was about 15% faster, people using the orthodox version couldn't effectively compete. Something had to be done. Finally, this new stroke—now known as the "butterfly"—won recognition as the fourth swimming stroke, and became an Olympic event in 1956.

The innovator is constantly challenging the rules. Most people will say, "As a rule, if operation 'XYZ' is done a certain way, it will get these results 'alpha-beta-gamma'." Here, 'XYZ' can be a marketing strategy, an engineering process, an accounting system, a package design, etc. The innovator will play with "XYZ" and will look for results *outside* the usual rules and guidelines.

One of my clients, an information display device manufacturer, has gone so far as to incorporate this philosophy into their motto:

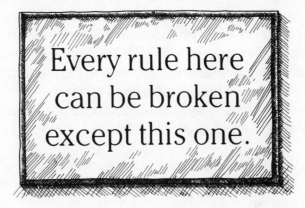

Every rule here
can be broken
except this one.

They feel that if they are following the same rules five years from now, then they won't have advanced the state of their art.

Follow The Rules

Playing the revolutionary is easier said than done. One company president told me that his most difficult problem is getting his subordinates to challenge the rules. He raises a good point. Why do people treat most problems and situations as closed ones with set rules, rather than as open ones which can be played with?

One main reason is that there is a lot of pressure in our culture to *follow the rules.* This value is one of the first things we learn as children. We are told, "Don't color outside the lines," and "No orange elephants." Our educational system encourages further rule-following. Students are usually better rewarded for regurgitating information than for playing with ideas and thinking of original uses for things. As a consequence, people feel more comfortable following the rules than challenging them.

From a practical standpoint, this value makes sense; in order to survive in society, we have to follow all kinds of rules. Shouting in a library or crying out "fire" in a packed theater are two things *not* to do. If, however, you are trying to generate new ideas, then the value "follow the rules" can be a mental lock because it means "think of things only as they are."

The Aslan Phenomenon

Challenging the rules is a good creative thinking strategy, but that's not all. Never challenging the rules brings with it at least two potential dangers. The first is that a person can get locked into one approach or method without seeing that other approaches might be more appropriate. As a result, he may tailor his problems to the preconceptions which enable him to solve them that way.

The other reason that the rules should be challenged is the "Aslan Phenomenon," which is as follows:

1. We make rules based on reasons that make a lot of sense.

2. We follow these rules.

3. Time passes, and things change.

4. The original reasons for the generation of these rules may no longer exist, but because the rules are still in place, we continue to follow them.

For example, I like to run, and I have three or four runs that I'll take depending on how far I want to go. One of these is a route which goes through my neighborhood for about four miles. As a rule, the run ends about two blocks from our house, because two years ago, when I started this route, there was a big, friendly golden retriever living at the house where I stopped. His name was Aslan. After my run, I would take some time to pet him and cool down. So stopping at Aslan's house became the rule for having a nice ending to a fun run.

But things have changed. His owner moved away a year ago, and took Aslan with her. Nevertheless, whenever I take this route, I still stop at the same place—even though Aslan no longer lives there. There are probably more pleasurable places to end my run, but because I'm following an obsolete rule, I haven't looked for them.

Here's another example of the Aslan phenomenon. Take a look at the following configuration of letters:

QWERTYUIOP

Are you familiar with them? You have undoubtedly seen this pattern many times. It is the top row of letters on a standardly configured typewriter keyboard. It is known as the QWERTY configuration, and it has a fascinating history.

Back in the 1870's, Sholes & Co., the leading manufacturer of typewriters at the time, received many complaints from users about the typewriter keys sticking together if the operator went too fast. In response, top management asked its engineers to figure out a way to prevent this from happening. The engineers discussed the problem for a while until one of them said, "What if we slowed the operator down? If we did that, the keys wouldn't jam together nearly as much. How can we slow the operator down?" One answer was to have a fairly inefficient keyboard configuration. For example, the letters "O" and "I" are the third and sixth most frequently used letters in the English alphabet, and yet the engineers positioned them on the keyboard so that the relatively weaker ring and little fingers had to depress them. This logic pervaded the keyboard, and this brilliant idea solved the problem.

Since that solution, the state of the art in typewriter and word processing technology has advanced significantly. There are now typewriters which can go much faster than any human operator can type. The problem is that the QWERTY configuration continues to be used even though there are faster configurations available. Once a rule gets in place, it's very difficult to eliminate it even though the original reason for its generation has gone away.

Summary

Creative thinking is not only constructive, it's also destructive. You often have to break out of one pattern to discover another one. So be responsive to change and be flexible with the rules. Remember, breaking the rules won't necessarily lead to creative ideas, but it's one avenue. And staying on the same road may eventually lead to a dead end. After all, many rules outlive the purpose for which they were intended.

☐ *TIP #7:* Play the revolutionary and challenge the rules—especially the ones you use to govern your day-to-day activities.

☐ ***TIP #8:*** Remember that playing the revolutionary also has its dangers. One man told me that whenever he gets bored with a routine, he likes to throw a "perturbation" into it to make it interesting. When he and his wife were in their mid-40's, they got bored with what they were doing and decided to have another child. Looking back on that decision, he says, "I think we over-perturbated."

☐ ***TIP #9:*** Periodically inspect your ideas to see if they are contributing to your thinking effectiveness. Ask yourself, "Why did this program, project, concept, or idea come to be?" And then follow this question with, "Do these reasons still exist?" If the answer is "no," eliminate the idea.

☐ ***TIP #10:*** Avoid falling in love with ideas. I got this advice several years ago from my printer. He said, "Don't fall in love with a particular type style, because if you do, you'll want to use it everywhere—even in places where it's inappropriate." I think that the same applies to ideas. I've seen people fall in love with a certain approach or system, and then be unable to see the merits of alternative approaches. I think one of life's great thrills is falling out of love with a previously cherished idea. When that happens, you're free to look for new ones.

☐ ***TIP #11:*** Have rule-inspecting and rule-discarding sessions within your organization. You may even find some motivational side benefits in this activity—finding and eliminating outmoded rules can be a lot of fun. Perhaps Mark Twain had something like this in mind when he said, "One of life's most over-valued pleasures is sexual intercourse; and, one of life's least appreciated pleasures is defecation."

4. "Be Practical."

Exercise: Imagine what would happen if gravity stopped for one second every day? What would things be like? What would land surfaces look like? How about the oceans and rivers? How would life have developed under such conditions? Would living things have special "zero-gravity adaptive features?" How would houses be designed? Imagine your living room. How would you design it and its furnishings if gravity stopped for one second every day?

Our Germinal Seedbed

Human beings occupy a special niche in the order of things. Because we have the ability to symbolize our experience, our thinking is not limited to the real and the present. This capability empowers our thinking in two major ways. First, it enables us to anticipate the future. We're able to ask ourselves: "Suppose it rains tomorrow? What would happen to our picnic? What alternative arrangements should be made?" By simulating such possibilities in your mind, we can plan for the future.

Second, since our thinking is not bound by real world constraints, we can generate ideas which have no correlate in the world of experience. You did this in the exercise about gravity. Similarly, you do it when you dream or imagine anything that doesn't actually exist.

I call the realm of the possible our "germinal seedbed." There are a lot of good soft thinking tools for cultivating this seedbed. In this chapter, we'll focus on two of them: the "what-if" question and the "stepping stone."

What-If

Asking "what-if" is an easy way to get your imagination going. To do it, you simply ask "what-if?" and then finish the question with some contrary-to-fact condition, idea, or situation.

What-if _____ ?

The what-if question can be whatever you wish, just as long as it is not a currently existing situation. The nice thing about "what-iffing" is that it allows you to suspend a few rules and assumptions, and get into a germinal frame of mind. A few examples:

☞ What-if animals became more intelligent than people?

☞ What-if human life-expectancy were 200 years?

☞ What-if bacteria which defecated petroleum were developed?

☞ What-if when you looked in the mirror, there became two of you?

☞ What-if everybody in your company played a musical instrument, and you had a concert every Friday afternoon at 3 o'clock?

☞ What-if people didn't need to sleep?

You can see that just asking the what-if question is not only a lot of fun; it also gives you the freedom to think something different.

Now, after you ask the what-if question, answer it.

What-if we had seven fingers on each hand?

Would we be able to wave and point at the same time? Would we have two finger-opposing thumbs on each hand? If we did, would we have a better "grasp" on things?

How would this affect sports? How would we

catch balls? Would we be more sure-handed?
Can't you just see some players, after a good play,
saying, "Gimme 7, gimme 14." That raises an interesting point: maybe our number system would
be base 14 instead of base 10. What kind of piano
music would be written if people had fourteen fingers? What would our hand tools look like? How
about our typewriter keyboards? How would they
be arranged? Would there be more shift keys?
Maybe instead of a keyboard there would be "key-
spheres"—balls with keys on them which you
squeezed to get the letters you wanted.

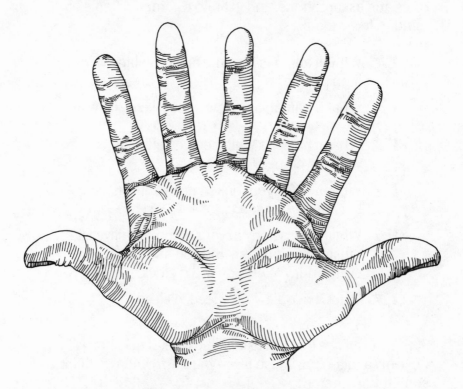

At the very least, this question makes us think about something we take for granted—our fingers.

The results of such seemingly playful speculation
need not be playful at all. A noted scientist once asked himself, "What-if I were falling through space in an elevator at
the speed of light, and there were a hole in the side of the
elevator? What-if a shaft of light came through this hole into
the elevator? What would happen?" By investigating the
ramifications of such a possibility, Albert Einstein developed some of his early relativity concepts.

Who should whack himself with this soft thinking tool? Everybody—housewives, salesmen, children, comedians, managers, doctors, florists, and you can all benefit from asking what-if. It's a way of freeing yourself from the deeply ingrained assumptions you have about your work.

I've known designers who would ask themselves questions such as, "What-if we made our products uglier and less reliable?" I've known engineers who tried to imagine "how something would function without one of its main parts" just to see what would happen. I've even seen a person try to rethink the toaster by asking, "What-if *I* were a toaster? How would I receive bread? What would it be like when my heating elements went on? What happens when caraway seeds fall to the bottom?" Now that's involving yourself in the problem!

The real key to asking what-if is allowing yourself to probe the possible, the impossible, and even the impractical for ideas. After all, you're only limited by your imagination; in the germinal phase, anything goes.

Try playing the magician (a magician is a person specializing in the fantasy what-if). This is an opportunity for you to speculate, and in the process, spawn some new ideas.

The Stepping Stone

What-if questions by themselves may not produce practical, creative ideas. Thus, it may be necessary to use another germinal thinking tool—the stepping stone. Stepping stones are simply provocative ideas which stimulate us to think about other ideas. Stepping stones may be impractical or improbable, but their value consists not in how practical they are, but in where they lead your thinking. Remember, when you are in the germinal phase, real world constraints don't apply. It often happens that an impractical idea leads to a practical, creative one. The following story is a good example of this phenomenon.

Several years ago, an engineer at a large chemical company asked the following question: "What if we put gunpowder in our house paint?" The people around him were somewhat taken aback, but the engineer continued.

Have you ever noticed what happens to paint after it's been on a house for three or four years? It chips and cracks and is very difficult to remove. There has to be a better way to get it off. If we put gunpowder in our house paint, we could just blow it right off the house.

The engineer had an interesting idea, but it had one drawback—it wasn't very practical.

The people who were listening to this man, however, did something very much to their credit. They didn't evaluate his idea on the basis of its practical merits. On the contrary, they approached it as a stepping stone which might lead them to a practical, creative idea. They thought, "What other ways are there to create a chemical reaction which would remove old house paint?" This question opened up their thinking and eventually led to the idea of putting additives in the house paint. These additives would be inert until another solution containing other additives was applied to the old paint at a later date. At this point, a reaction would take place between the two sets of additives that would cause the paint to strip right off. That company is currently working on making such a paint removal process a reality.

Funny Trash

A few years ago, a city in the Netherlands had a refuse problem. A once-clean section of town had become an eyesore because people had stopped using the trash cans. There were cigarette butts, beer bottles, chocolate wrappers, newspapers, and other trash littering the streets.

Obviously, the sanitation department was concerned, so they sought ways to clean up the city. One idea was to double the littering fine from 25 guilders to 50 guilders for each offense. They tried this, but it had little effect. Another approach was to increase the number of litter-agents who patrolled the area. This was more of the same, that is, another "punish the litterer" solution, and it, too, had little impact on the problem.

Then somebody asked the following question:

> What-if our trash cans paid people money when they put their trash in? We could put an electronic sensing device on each can as well as a coin-return mechanism. Whenever a person put trash in the can, it would pay him 10 guilders.

This idea, to say the least, whacked everyone's thinking. The what-iffer had changed the situation from a "punish the litterer" problem to a "reward the law-abider" problem. The idea had one glaring fault, however; if the city implemented the idea, it would go bankrupt.

Fortunately, the people who were listening to this idea didn't evaluate it based on its practical merits. Instead, they used it as a stepping stone and asked themselves, "What other ways are there in which we can reward people for putting their trash in the trash cans?" This question led to the following solution. The sanitation department developed electronic trash cans which had a sensing unit on the top which would detect when a piece of refuse had been deposited. This would activate a tape-recorder that would play a recording of a joke. In other words, joke-telling trash cans! Different trash cans told different kinds of jokes (some told bad puns while others told shaggy dog stories) and soon developed reputations. The jokes were changed every two weeks. As a result, people went out of their way to put their trash in the trash cans, and the town became clean once again. (For those of you who are interested, that is the origin of the comedy term "throw-away line.")

The point is this: you don't execute stepping stones, you launch your thinking from them. Indeed, there are some creative ideas which can only be reached through a stepping stone or two.

Be Practical

Why don't people use what-if thinking and stepping stones more often to generate ideas? There are several reasons. One is that as people grow older, they become prisoners of familiarity. They get used to the "what-is" of reality and forget about the possibilities that asking "what-if" can generate.

A second reason is that these tools are low-probability in character; it is fairly unlikely that any given what-if question will produce a practical, creative idea. Thus, you may have to ask many what-if questions and follow out many stepping stones before reaching a practical creative idea. How many what-if questions did Einstein ask himself before he boarded his imaginary elevator? A hundred? Two hundred? No matter. He eventually got a good idea which he probably wouldn't have gotten had he stayed in the practical realm. Thus, even though the likelihood of any given what-if question reaching fruition is low, a few germinal ideas will bear fruit in the world of action. Most people, however, don't feel they have the time to do this, so they limit themselves to the more practical what-is.

The third reason we don't use these tools is that we haven't been taught to. What happens to our imaginations as we mature? When we are young, they are cultivated in fairy tales and imagination games, but then we are told to "grow up." One of my workshop participants had this appraisal:

The amount a person uses his imagination is inversely proportional to the amount of punishment he will receive for using it.

Her implication: it's okay for children but not for adults to spend their time what-iffing. We have been trained to respond to unusual ideas by saying, "That's not practical," instead of, "Hey, that's interesting; I wonder where it will lead our thinking." The danger of premature evaluation is that nothing will be conceived. If the people who were discussing the possibility of "gunpowder paint" or "coin-return trash cans" had said, "Be Practical," they never would have given themselves an opportunity to take a germinal idea and turn it into a usable one.

To be sure, you need to be practical for almost all of your daily activities. If you aren't, you probably won't survive very long. You can't live on imaginary food, or stop your car with "what-if brakes" that save brake lining by working only 75% of the time. Being practical is important in the world of action, but practicality alone will not generate new ideas. The logic which works so well in judging and executing ideas may stifle the creative process if it prevents the artist in you from exploring unusual germinal ideas.

Summary

This world was built by practical people who knew how to get into a germinal frame of mind, listen to their imaginations, and build on the ideas they found there.

☐ *TIP #12:* Each of you has an "artist" and a "judge" within you. The open-minded attitude of the artist typifies the kind of thinking you use in the germinal phase when you're generating ideas. The evaluative outlook of the judge represents the kind of thinking you use in the practical phase when preparing ideas for execution. I recommend that you avoid bringing in your judge before your artist has had a chance to do his job. Premature evaluation can prevent conception.

☐ *TIP #13:* Be a magician: ask "what-if" questions and use the provocative answers you find as stepping stones to new ideas.

☐ *TIP #14:* Cultivate your imagination. Set aside time every day to ask yourself what-if questions. Although the likelihood that any given "what-if" question will lead to a practical idea isn't high, the more often you practice this activity, the more productive you'll become.

☐ *TIP #15:* Encourage what-iffing in others. Many of my clients have established a "what-if question of the week" within their departments as a way of looking for potential problems and opportunities. "What-if the government changed its tax laws on capital depreciation?" "What-if the cost of money doubled in the next six months?" "What-if computer memory were free?" "What-if the market for our largest selling product shrank to 25% of its current size?" "What-if we only went to work three days a week and did the rest of the work at home?"

Breaktime.

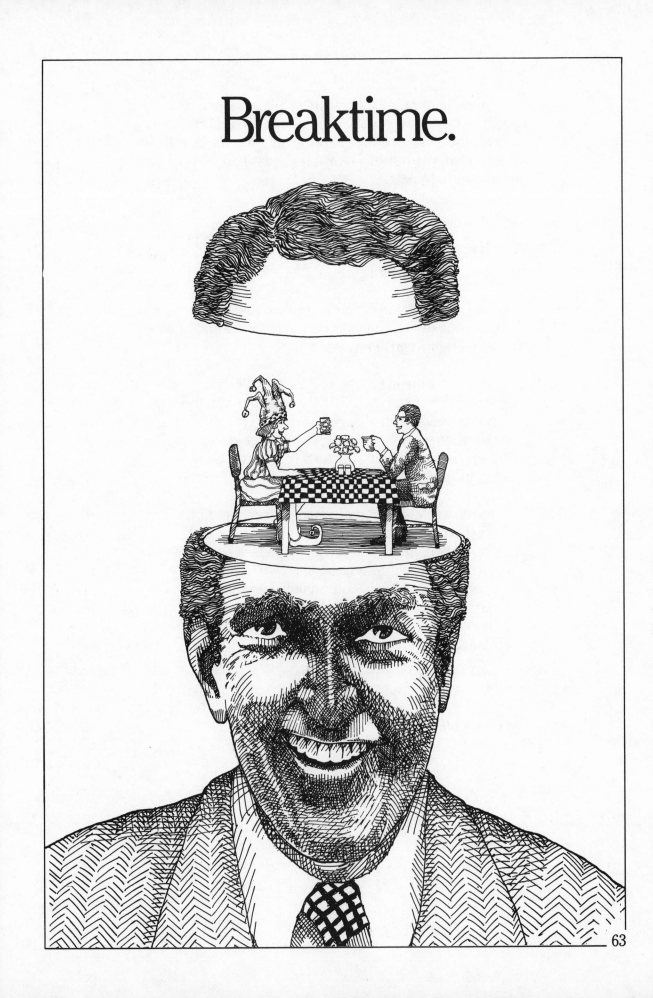

Opening mental locks is a lot of fun, but it can also make you work up a sweat, so let's take a break here. If you want to grab a cup of coffee or tea, or take a walk, go right ahead. When you return, I have a few ideas I hope you'll enjoy taking a look at.

Reverse Living

Here is one person's view of what would happen if we lived our lives backwards.

Life is tough. It takes up a lot of your time, all your weekends, and what do you get at the end of it?…Death, a great reward.

I think that the life cycle is all backwards. You should die first, get it out of the way, then you live twenty years in an old age home. You get kicked out when you're too young, you get a gold watch, you go to work. You work forty years until you're young enough to enjoy your retirement.

You go to college, you do drugs, you do alcohol, you party, until you're ready for high school. You go to high school, you go to grade school, you become a little kid, you play, you have no responsibilities, you become a little baby, you go back into the womb, you spend your last nine months floating, and you finish off as a gleam in somebody's eye.

Puzzle

Exercise: Connect the dots.

.
1

.
2

TIP : For more effective thinking, rotate your ideas every 10,000 thoughts. Creativity involves not only generating new ideas, but escaping from obsolete ones as well.

NEW IDEA

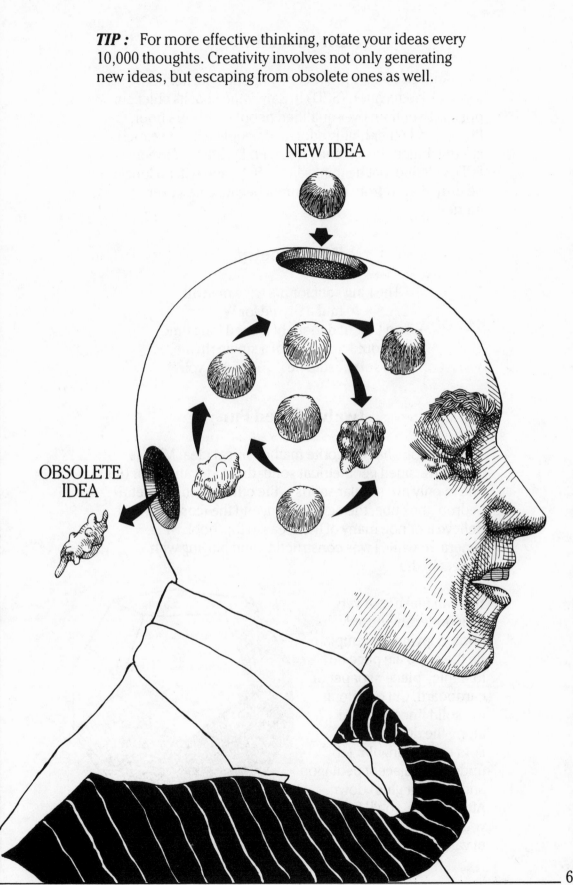

OBSOLETE
IDEA

Diseducation

Andrew Mercer has recently opened the Sequoia College of Diseducation (SCD) in San Francisco. Its chief purpose is to untrain over-qualified people. This is a boon to Ph.D.'s and other highly educated people who are experiencing difficulties getting jobs. A Ph.D., after four years at SCD, will find that he thinks like a B.A., and will no longer be turned away from employment because he's overtrained.

Royal Poetry

The king sent for his wise men all
To find a rhyme for W;
When they had thought a good long time
But could not think of a single rhyme,
"I'm sorry," said he, "To trouble you."

Twelve-Sided Fun

Everyone has a favorite mathematical idea. Mine is the twelve-sided geometrical solid, the dodecahedron. (It's one of only five regular solids—the others being the tetrahedron, the cube, the octohedron, and the icosahedron.) Believe it or not, many of the ideas in this book were generated while I was constructing and playing with dodecahedra.

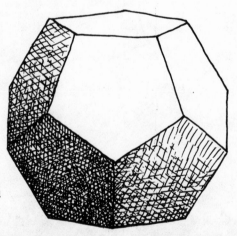

You can make your very own dodecahedron by photocopying the template on the opposite page on to a thick piece of paper or cardboard. Cut out along the solid lines and fold along the dotted lines. Fold each triangular tab under the adjacent pentagon and tape (or glue) down. After awhile, you'll have your own dodecahedron to play with. You might even think of various things to put on the different sides.

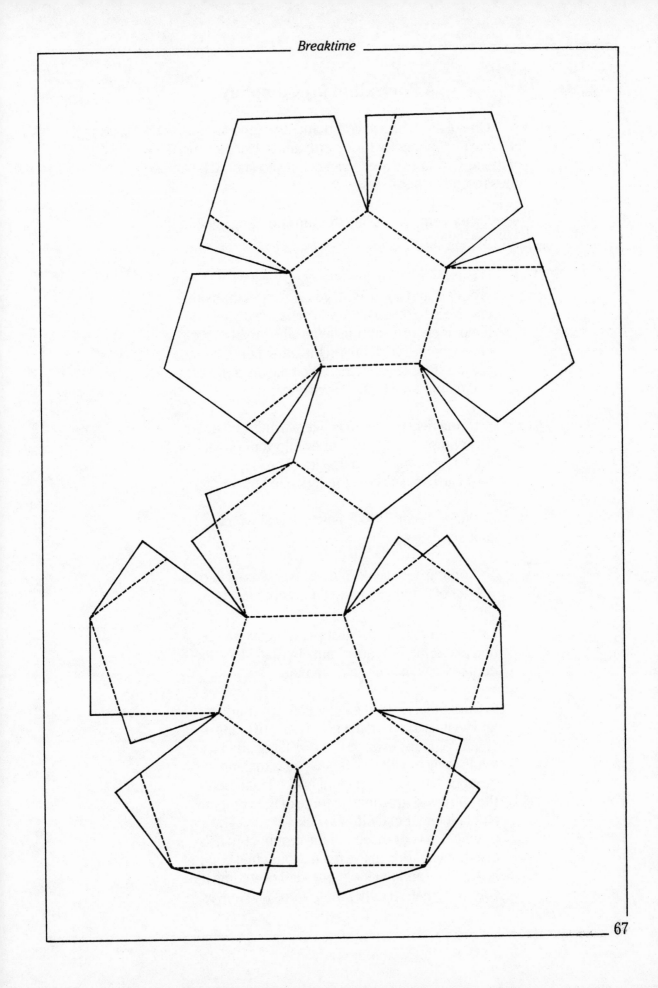

A Portrait of My Company

One of the exercises participants in my workshops do is make metaphors for their companies. Here are just a few of them. The names aren't given, but you should be able to guess some of them.

☆Our company is like the sun shedding light on the data processing world.

☆Our company is like a winery. We have different products and some vintages are better than others. We also have two kinds of users: on the one hand, there are connoisseurs who greatly appreciate what we've done; on the other hand, there are the "Ripple drinkers" who take our software and manipulate to their own ends.

☆Doing research here is like playing stud poker. The company will put money into your project as long as your hand shows a lot of promise or the next card doesn't cost too much to buy.

☆Our company is like a maze looking for a mouse.

☆Working here is like a nightmare. You'd like to get out of it, but you need the sleep.

☆Our company is like a supertanker. It's large and powerful, but moves slowly. Also, once the course is set, it's tough to change.

☆Our company is like Peter Pan. It's childlike, and wishes to retain the good parts of being a small company even as it grows larger. Being made to fly is a kind of fantasy as is making the best product. Our president is like Tinkerbell—the spirit and imaginative force of the company. Our chief financial officer is like Wendy—he's practical, has both feet on the ground, but he's also pulled along in the magic. Our chief competitor is like Captain Hook; but we'll overcome him with imagination rather than "guns and knives."

☆Our company is like a three-ring circus with marketing, R&D, and manufacturing each trying to occupy the center ring. The president is the ring master. Marketing has the high wire act, R&D has the magic act, and manufacturing are the elephants. Advertising is in charge of ticket sales; customer support are the peanut vendors; the customers are the audience; the field engineers are the clowns between the rings; and, the grand finale is when we successfully install a system that works.

☆Our company is like a galley ship without a drummer. We've got some people rowing at full beat, some at one-half beat, some at one-quarter beat, and some dead beats. Also, the captain is steering by the wake.

☆Working here is like urinating in a dark suit. It's warm and it feels good but it doesn't show.

☆Our company is like a giant human body. Administration is the guts. Sales and marketing are the mouth. Corporate management is the mind making decisions. Research and development is the reproductive system. And the secretaries and the technicians are the skeleton that supports the body.

Generations

Historians say that there are three generations in a century. In my case, that is exactly correct. I was born on February 16, 1948, one century to the day after my great grandfather, Peter, who was born on February 16, 1848. I seem to be keeping up the pattern, too. My daughter, Athena, was born on June 16, 1981, exactly one-third of a century to the day after me.

The Man With The Smelly Mind

We often hear about people with "clear" minds. This reflects the "optical view" of knowledge (cf. "That's Not Logical"). What if, instead of sight, we used the olfactory sense to describe the mind? In that case, it would be possible for a person to have a "smelly mind."

Intellectual Popcorn

☆Only the most foolish of mice would hide in a cat's ear. But only the wisest of cats would think to look there.
Andrew Mercer

☆The yellow pad is the blank canvas of the businessman.
Bill Ghormley

☆Most advances in science come when a person for one reason or another is forced to change fields.
Peter Borden

☆There are two kinds of truth, small truth and great truth. You can recognize a small truth because its opposite is a falsehood. The opposite of a great truth is another truth.
Niels Bohr

☆You can't top pigs with pigs.
Walt Disney

☆The only person who likes change is a wet baby.
Roy Z-M Blitzer

☆For those of you who consider life to be a joke, consider the punch line.
Anon.

☆The society which scorns excellence in plumbing because it is a humble activity and tolerates shoddiness in philosophy because it is in exalted activity will have neither good plumbing nor good philosophy. Neither its pipes nor its theories will hold water.
John W. Gardner

☆Can a blue man sing the whites?
Algis Juodikis

☆There are three ways to get to the top of a tree: 1) climb it; 2) sit on an acorn; or, 3) make friends with a big bird.
Robert Maidment

High Productivity

Under Soviet economic rules, the productivity of a factory is measured not by how many units it produces, but by how much material it consumes. As a consequence, the link between worker and productivity is broken. Such a policy can have bizarre results—at least in terms of how it motivates people.

The managers of a factory that manufactures metal camping ware and frying pans realized that if they used more metal, they would get bonuses for exceeding plan. The workers, however, did not want to increase their output. How to get around the dilemma? They decided to produce heavier camping ware. Soon the factory was earning bonuses, while hapless campers were getting strained backs.

Colorful Concepts

Have you ever noticed how colorful our language is? There are all kinds of concepts which are described by colors. For example:

Red Tape   Green Thumb   Rednecks

Gray Matter   Yellow Fever   Green Belts

Silver Linings   Blue Laws

White Noise   Black Holes   Blackmail

Blackball   Blue Moon   Greenbacks

White Elephants   Yellow Streak

Blue Bloods   Red Alert

Whitewash   Greenhorns   Black Magic

Golden Rule   White Papers   Blue Notes

Red Undancy   Blue Chip

Four Advertising Ideas

When everyone else zigs, zag.
Tom Yobaggy

Afflict the comfortable.
Carl Ally

It's better to have a philosophy to out-think your competition than to outspend them.
Les Wolff

Rules are for the obedience of fools and the guidance of wise men.
David Ogilvy

Jack Grimes's Software Joke

Software Manager: I like your program except for the ending.

Programmer: What's wrong with the ending?

Software Manager: It should be closer to the beginning.

Well, the break's over now—hope you got some ideas.

Let's open another lock!

5. "Avoid Ambiguity."

Exercise: In the following line of letters, cross out six letters so that the remaining letters without altering their sequence, will spell a familiar English word.

B S A I N X L E A T N T E A R S

Play with it for a while before proceeding.

Thinking Ambiguously

In the mid-1960's, former FBI director J. Edgar Hoover was reading a typed copy of a letter he had just dictated to his secretary. He didn't like the way she had formatted the letter, so he wrote on the bottom, "Watch the borders," and asked her to re-type it. The secretary did as she was instructed and sent it off to all the top agents. For the next two weeks FBI agents were put on special alert along the Canadian and Mexican borders.

This story illustrates two of the main reasons why most people don't like ambiguous situations (those that can be interpreted in more than one way); they're confusing, and they cause communication problems. As a result, we have learned to *avoid ambiguity.* This is a good rule to follow for most practical situations such as giving directions, documenting programs, or drawing up contracts. On these occasions, it's important to be clear, precise, and specific in order to get your message across.

There are instances, however, when ambiguity can be a powerful stimulant to your imagination. When you're in the germinal phase of the creative process, a little ambiguity can whack you into asking such questions as,

What's going on?
What does this mean?
How else can it be interpreted?

These are special questions, the kind you ask when you're looking for new ideas. So, one way to find the second right answer is to look at things ambiguously. For example, what is half of 8? One answer is 4. But if you assume that the question is ambiguous, you'll look for other answers such as 0, 3, E, M, and "eig," all depending on how you define "half."

Exercise: What is this figure?

If you look at it one way, it's a bird; if you look at it another way, it could be a question mark; if you turn it upside down, it looks like a seal juggling a ball on its nose. By assuming an ambiguous attitude, you generate a variety of ideas.

Okay, how did you do with the six letter exercise? What word did you find? Many people look at the problem and say, "Okay, here's a string of 16 letters, and to solve this problem I should cross out 6 of them. That means I'm looking for a 10 letter word." And that's what they spend their time looking for.

I gave this problem to a man who owned a computer. He went home that night and said, "I'll show that Roger. I'll write a program to cross out 6 letters, and have the computer figure out the answer. I'll just take a shower while it does this, and when I get back, the answer will be printed out." When he came back, he had a roll of printout thirty feet long containing such glittering possible solutions as:

```
SAINXEAEAR    BSAIXEEARS    BSINLEANEA
BINXLTEARS    AINXLEANAS    BANEATNTER
SINXEATNTE    BAINLATNAR    SNLETNTARS
SANLATNTAR    INXLEANEAR    INXEATEARS
BSNXLENTAR    INLETNTARS    SAIXNTEARS
SANXATNTEA    SINXLETERS    SAILTNTEAR
NLEATNTEAS    IXLEATNTAS    SAINLATEAR
IXLEATTEAR    BIXLETTEAR    BAINEATARS
SNXLETTEAR    BSNLENEARS    INEATNTEAR
BSAXLETARS    BLEATTEARS    INXATNTEAR
BAINNEANRS    SXLEATNTES    BINLATTEAR
SINLETNEAR    SIXATNTEAS    BSXLETTEAS
SNXLEATNRS    ANXLEATNAS    AINLTNTEAR
BAINXATEAR    BAXLEATEAR    BSIXLANERS
```

As soon as he saw this list, he realized that he had
been asking the computer the wrong question. He discovered that you can have the greatest computer on earth, but
if you've got the wrong program in it, you'll end up with
garbage.

One way to solve this problem is to interpret the in-
structions with an ambiguous attitude. What else could
"cross out six letters" mean? Perhaps, instead of crossing
out 6 letters, you literally crossed out the "S," and the "I,"
and the "X," and the "L," and the "E," and so on. If you try
this approach, you will be left with the word:

BANANA

My point is this: if you want to find the second right
answer, try looking at things ambiguously. The kindergartners who saw the chalk dot as an owl's eye, a cigar butt, a
bean, and other things had the ability to do this. So did
Picasso when he saw the bicycle handle-bars as bull's
horns. And so do you if you've ever used a brick as a door
stop, made chimes out of forks and spoons, used leaves
as toilet paper, or used a ball point pen as a hole punch.
The ability to find ambiguity is an important part of thinking
something different.

NOTE: Since this book is advocating looking for the second right answer, I should point
out that there is at least one other solution to this problem. If you choose six different
letters—say "B," "S," "A," "I," "N," and "X"—and cross them out every time they appear,
you would end up with the word "LETTER."

The Wooden Wall

Here's another example of how ambiguity can have a stimulating effect on your thinking—if you're receptive to it. Probably the most famous source of ambiguous pronouncements was the oracle at Delphi in the ancient world. One of the oracle's best known prophecies came in the year 480 B.C. The Persians under Xerxes had invaded the Greek mainland and had successfully conquered two-thirds of the country. Naturally, the Athenian city-fathers were concerned as to which course of action they should take against the on-coming Persians. They realized, however, that before any decision could be made, they should send some suppliants to Delphi to get a reading from the oracle. The suppliants made the journey and received the following prophecy:

The wooden wall will save you and your children.

The suppliants took these words back to Athens. At first, the city-fathers were unsure what the prophecy meant. Then one peron suggested that they should build a wooden wall up on the Acropolis and take a defensive stand behind it. That's what the "wooden wall" meant—a barricade on the Acropolis. His interpretation made a lot of sense.

But the city-fathers knew that the oracle was intentionally ambiguous so that they would be forced to go beyond the first right answer. They tried to think of all of the contexts

—both literal and metaphorical—in which the words "the wooden wall will save you and your children" would make sense. After some thought, they came up with an-

other idea. Could the "wooden wall" the oracle was referring to be the result of all of the Athenian wooden-hulled ships lined up next to one another? From a distance, the ships would indeed look like a wooden wall. The city-fathers decided, therefore, that the battle should be a naval one rather than a land one.

In 479 B.C., the Athenians went on to rout the Persians in the Battle of Salamis. Here, the oracle's ambiguity forced the Athenians to consult the wisdom of their own intuition, and consider alternatives.

General George S. Patton had similar ideas on how to stimulate people's creativity. He said, "If you tell people where to go, but not how to get there, you'll be amazed at the results." He knew that posing a problem in an ambiguous way would give more freedom to the imaginations of the people who were working on the problem.

The renowned architect Arthur Erickson also uses this same strategy to unlock his students' creativity. Here's an example of one of his exercises. Give it a try.

Exercise: Draw a picture of yourself in a position of movement, and then provide a device (made out of plastic, wood, paper, or metal) to support that position.

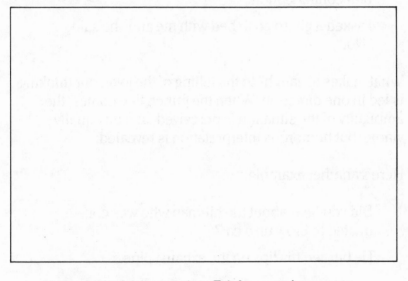

At the end of the exercise, Erickson points out to his students that they had been designing furniture. As he puts it,

> If I had said to the students, "Look, we're going to design a chair or a bed," they would have explored the design on the basis of previous memories of chairs or beds. But by approaching the model from the opposite and essential direction, I was able to make them realize the vital aspects of furniture.

As you can see, often all you need is a dose or two of ambiguity to whack your thinking into high gear. Thus, I'd like to prescribe a few of the following sources of ambiguity to you.

Humor

Did you hear about the man who had a pre-frontal lobotomy? He changed his mind.

Most humorists are exposers of ambiguity; they show you something you usually think of in one way and then present you with another possible interpretation. To understand most jokes, you have to see the ambiguity of the situation presented. Here is a Woody Allen example:

I'd like to say just a word about "oral contraception." I was involved in a very good example of oral contraception.

I asked a girl to go to bed with me and she said, "No."

What makes us laugh? In the telling of the joke, our thinking is led in one direction. When the punch line comes, the ambiguity of the situation is perceived, and an equally viable, but humorous interpretation is revealed.

Here's another example:

Did you hear about the hit-man who was contracted to blow up a car?

He burned his lips on the exhaust pipe.

Try using humor to put yourself in a creative state of mind. One way I have found to be effective is to listen to about an hour's worth of comedy records. Another way is to settle down in the couch with a few cartoon books. After doing either activity, I'm in a good frame of mind to think something different.

Paradoxes

This chapter is paradoxical. On the one hand, I've said that ambiguity causes communication problems. On the other, I've said that it helps to create new ideas. What's the common denominator? Both situations stimulate people to think.

That's probably the reason why, in the midst of a difficult problem, the physicist Niels Bohr was overheard to say, "How wonderful that we have met with a paradox. Now we have some hope of making some progress." Bohr knew that paradoxes are crucial to the creative process. That's because they whack you out of narrow thought paths, and force you to question your assumptions. Indeed, the very act of "seeing the paradox" is at the crux of creative thinking—the ability to entertain two different (and often contradictory) notions at the same time.

I'd like to share some of my favorite paradoxes with you:

☞ Be spontaneous!

☞ The little I know I owe to my ignorance.

☞ There is nothing so unthinkable as thought unless it be the entire absence of thought.
Samuel Butler

☞ Mr. Smith was disappointed to find no suggestion box in the clubhouse because he would like to put a suggestion in it about having one.

☞ Only the ephemeral is of lasting value. *Ionesco*

☞ A physicist is an atom's way of knowing about atoms. *George Wald*

☞ We can't leave the haphazard to chance.
N.F. Simpson

☞ The notes I handle no better than many pianists. But the pauses between notes—ah, that is where the art resides! *Schnabel*

☞ A bank will lend you money only if you prove you don't need it.

☞ Art is a lie that makes us realize the truth.
Picasso

Heraclitus

Finally, I believe that everyone should have their own personal source of ambiguity. This could be a person, a book, a thing—whatever—that forces you to look for more than one meaning in order to understand what's going on. One of mine is the ancient Greek philosopher Heraclitus who lived about the fifth century B.C. Even to his contemporaries he was known as the "Obscure One." Here are some of his thoughts:

☞ Everything flows.

☞ It is not possible to step into the same river twice.

☞ Sea water is the purest and most polluted: for fish it is drinkable and life-giving; for men, not drinkable and destructive.

☞ They do not understand how that which differs with itself is in agreement: harmony consists of opposing tension, like that of the lyre and the bow.

☞ The way up and the way down are one and the same.

☞ If all things turned to smoke, the nose would be the discriminating organ.

☞ If you don't expect the unexpected you will not find it, for it is not to be reached by search or trail.

☞ To those who are awake, there is one ordered universe common to all, whereas in sleep each man turns away from this world to one of his own.

☞ There await men after they are dead things which they do not expect or imagine.

☞ Time is a child playing draughts: the kingship is in the hands of the child.

☞ It is not good for men to achieve all they wish.

☞ Man is most nearly himself when he achieves the seriousness of a child at play.

☞ A man's character is his destiny.

☞ I searched into myself.

☞ Lovers of wisdom must be inquirers into very many things indeed.

I've been reading Heraclitus for over fifteen years, and he never fails to stimulate my thinking.

I suggest that you seek out your own source of ambiguity and cultivate it as a valuable resource. It should be clear by now that idea-generation is not the accident most people believe it to be. You _can_ improve your idea-having average with such tools.

Summary

Most of us have learned to "avoid ambiguity" because of the communication problems it can cause. This is an especially good idea in practical situations where the consequences of such a misunderstanding would be serious. For example, a firechief fighting a three-alarm fire needs to issue his orders with utmost clarity so as to leave nothing to question.

In germinal situations, however, there is the danger that too much specificity can stifle your imagination. Let's suppose that the same firechief has asked you to paint a mural on the side of his firehouse. If he tells you exactly what he wants it to look like right down to the last detail, he hasn't given you any room to use your imagination. Perhaps, if the assignment were stated somewhat ambiguously, then you would have more room to think. In other words, there is a place for ambiguity—perhaps not so much when you're executing ideas, but certainly when you're searching for them.

☐ **_TIP #16:_** Take advantage of the ambiguity in the world. Look at something and think about what else it might be.

☐ **TIP #17:** If you're giving someone a problem that has the potential of being solved in a creative way, then you might try—at least initially—posing it in an ambiguous fashion so as to not restrict their imagination.

☐ **TIP #18:** Cultivate your own personal sources of ambiguity. These could be people, books, things—whatever—that force you to look for more than one meaning in order to understand what's going on.

☐ **TIP #19:** Try using humor to put you or your group in a creative state of mind.

☐ **TIP #20:** Write an ambiguous job description for yourself. What are 3 different ways it could be interpreted?

6. "To Err Is Wrong."

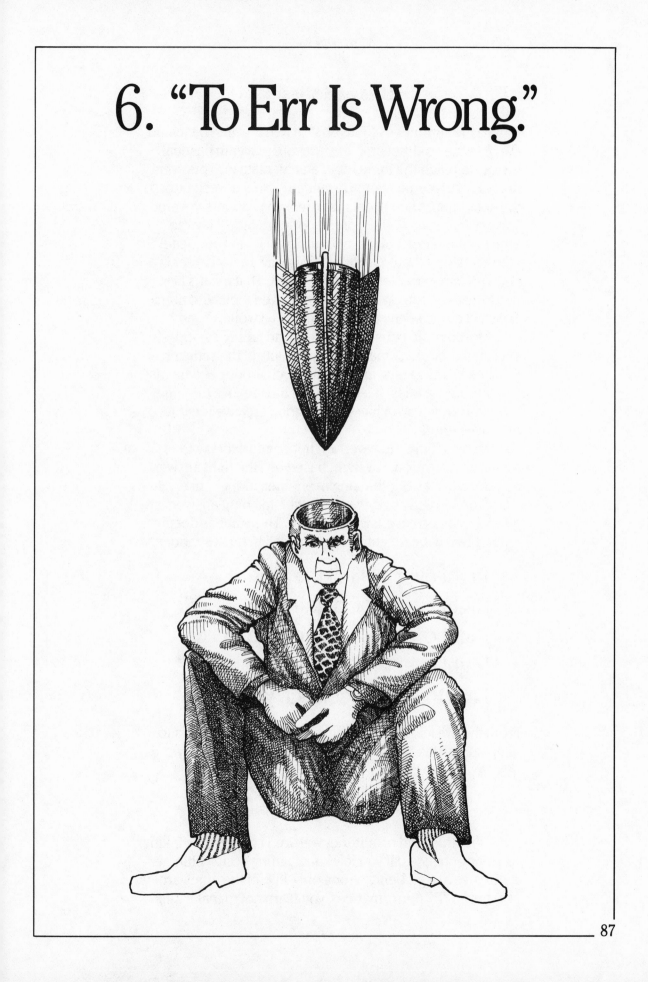

Hits and Misses

In the summer of 1979, Boston Red Sox first baseman Carl Yastrzemski became the fifteenth player in baseball history to reach the three thousand hit plateau. This event drew a lot of media attention, and for about a week prior to the attainment of this goal, hundreds of reporters covered Yaz's every move. Finally, one reporter asked, "Hey Yaz, aren't you afraid all of this attention will go to your head?" Yastrzemski replied, "I look at it this way: in my career I've been up to bat over ten thousand times. That means I've been unsuccessful at the plate over seven thousand times. That fact alone keeps me from getting a swollen head."

Most people consider success and failure as opposites, but they are actually both products of the same process. As Yaz suggests, an activity which produces a hit may also produce a miss. It is the same with creative thinking; the same energy which generates good creative ideas also produces errors.

Many people, however, are not comfortable with errors. Our educational system, based on "the right answer" belief, cultivates our thinking in another, more conservative way. From an early age, we are taught that right answers are good and incorrect answers are bad. This value is deeply embedded in the incentive system used in most schools:

Right over 90% of the time = "A"
Right over 80% of the time = "B"
Right over 70% of the time = "C"
Right over 60% of the time = "D"
Less than 60% correct, you fail.

From this we learn to be right as often as possible and to keep our mistakes to a minimum. We learn, in other words, that *"to err is wrong."*

Playing It Safe

With this kind of attitude, you aren't going to be taking too many chances. If you learn that failing even a little penalizes you (e.g., being wrong only 15% of the time garners you only a "B" performance), you learn not to make mistakes. And more important, you learn not to put yourself in situations where you might fail. This leads to conservative thought patterns designed to avoid the stigma our society puts on "failure."

I have a friend who recently graduated from college with a Master's degree in Journalism. For the last six months, she has been trying to find a job, but to no avail. I talked with her about her situation, and realized that her problem is that she doesn't know how to fail. She went through eighteen years of schooling without ever failing an examination, a paper, a midterm, a pop-quiz, or a final. Now, she is reluctant to try any approaches where she might fail. She has been conditioned to believe that failure is bad in and of itself, rather than a potential stepping stone to new ideas.

Look around. How many middle managers, house-wives, administrators, teachers, and other people do you see who are afraid to try anything new because of this fear of failure? Most of us have learned not to make mistakes in public. As a result, we remove ourselves from many learn-ing experiences except for those occurring in the most pri-vate of circumstances.

A Different Logic

From a practical point of view, "to err is wrong" makes sense. Our survival in the everyday world requires us to perform thousands of small tasks without failure. Think about it: you wouldn't last very long if you were to step out in front of traffic or stick your hand into a pot of boiling water. In addition, engineers whose bridges collapse, stock brokers who lose money for their clients and copywriters whose ad campaigns decrease sales won't keep their jobs very long.

Nevertheless, too great an adherence to the belief "to err is wrong" can greatly undermine your attempts to gener-ate new ideas. If you're more concerned with producing right answers than generating original ideas, you'll proba-bly make uncritical use of the rules, formulae, and proce-dures used to obtain these right answers. By doing this, you'll by-pass the germinal phase of the creative process, and thus spend little time testing assumptions, challenging the rules, asking what-if questions, or just playing around with the problem. All of these techniques will produce some incorrect answers, but in the germinal phase errors are viewed as a necessary by-product of creative thinking. As Yaz would put it, "If you want the hits, be prepared for the misses." That's the way the game of life goes.

Errors As Stepping Stones

Whenever an error pops up, the usual response is "Jeez, another screwup, what went wrong this time?" The creative thinker, on the other hand, will realize the potential value of errors, and perhaps say something like, "Would you look at that! Where can it lead our thinking?" And then he or she will go on to use the error as a stepping stone to a new idea. As a matter of fact, the whole history of discovery is filled with people who used erroneous assumptions and failed ideas as stepping stones to new ideas. Columbus thought he was finding a shorter route to India. Johannes Kepler stumbled on to the idea of interplanetary gravity because of assumptions which were right for the wrong reasons. And, Thomas Edison knew 1800 ways *not* to build a light bulb.

The following story about the automotive genius Charles Kettering exemplifies the spirit of working through erroneous assumptions to good ideas. In 1912, when the automobile industry was just beginning to grow, Kettering was interested in improving gasoline-engine efficiency. The problem he faced was "knock," the phenomenon in which gasoline takes too long to burn in the cylinder—thereby reducing efficiency.

Kettering began searching for ways to eliminate the "knock." He thought to himself, "How can I get the gasoline to combust in the cylinder at an earlier time?" The key concept here is "early." Searching for analogous situations, he looked around for models of "things that happen early." He thought of historical models, physical models, and biological models. Finally, he remembered a particular plant, the trailing arbutus, which "happens early," i.e., it blooms in the snow ("earlier" than other plants). One of this plant's chief characteristics is its red leaves which help the plant retain light at certain wavelengths. Kettering figured that it must be the red color which made the trailing arbutus bloom earlier.

Now came the critical step in Kettering's chain of thought. He asked himself, "How can I make the gasoline red? Perhaps I'll put red dye in the gasoline—maybe that'll make it combust earlier." He looked around his workshop, and found that he didn't have any red dye. But he did happen to have some iodine—perhaps that would do. He added the iodine to the gasoline and, lo and behold, the engine didn't "knock."

Several days later, Kettering wanted to make sure that it was the redness of the iodine which had in fact solved his problem. He got some red dye and added it to the gasoline. Nothing happened! Kettering then realized that it wasn't the "redness" which had solved the "knock" problem, but certain other properties of iodine. In this case, an error had proven to be a stepping stone to a better idea. Had he known that "redness" alone was not the solution, he may not have found his way to the additives in iodine.

Negative Feedback

Errors serve another useful purpose: they tell us when to change direction. When things are going smoothly, we generally don't think about them. To a great extent, this is because we function according to the principle of negative feedback. Often it is only when things or people fail to do their job that they get our attention. For example, you are probably not thinking about your kneecaps right now; that's because everything is fine with them. The same goes for your elbows: they are also performing their function—no problem at all. But if you were to break a leg, you would immediately notice all of the things you could no longer do, but which you used to take for granted.

Negative feedback means that the current approach is not working, and it is up to you to figure out a new one. We learn by trial and error, not by trial and rightness. If we did things correctly every time, we would never have to change direction—we'd just continue the current course and end up with more of the same.

For example, after the supertanker *Amoco Cadiz* broke up off the cost of Brittany in the spring of 1978, thereby polluting the coast with hundreds of thousands of tons of oil, the oil industry re-thought many of its safety standards regarding petroleum transport. The same thing happened after the accident at the Three Mile Island nuclear reactor in 1979—many procedures and safety standards were changed.

Neil Goldschmidt, former Secretary of Transportation, had this to say about the Bay Area Rapid Transit (BART):

> It's gotten too fashionable around the country to beat up on BART and not give credit to the vision that put this system in place. We have learned from BART around the country. The lessons were put to use in Washington, in Atlanta, in Buffalo, and other cities where we are building mass transit systems. One of the lessons is not to build a system like BART.

We learn by our failures. A person's errors are the whacks that lead him to think something different.

Trying New Things

Your error rate in any activity is a function of your familiarity with that activity. If you are doing things that are routine and have a high likelihood of correctness, then you will probably make very few errors. But if you are doing things that have no precedence in your experience or are trying different approaches, then you will be making your share of mistakes. Innovators may not bat a thousand—far from it—but they do get new ideas.

The creative director of an advertising agency told me that he isn't happy unless he is failing at least half of the time. As he puts it, "If you are going to be original, you are going to be wrong a lot."

One of my clients, the president of a fast-growing computer company, tells his people: "We're innovators. We're doing things nobody has ever done before. Therefore, we are going to be making mistakes. My advice to you: make your mistakes, but make them in a hurry."

Another client, a division manager of a high-technology company, asked his vice president of engineering what percentage of their new products should be successful in the marketplace. The answer he received was "about 50%." The division manager replied, "That's too high. 30% is a better target; otherwise we'll be too conservative in our planning."

Along similar lines, in the banking industry, it is said that if the credit manager never has to default on any of his loans, it's a sure sign he's not being aggressive enough in the marketplace.

Thomas J. Watson, the founder of IBM, has similar words: "The way to succeed is to double your failure rate."

Thus, errors, at the very least, are a sign that we are diverging from the main road and trying different approaches.

Nature's Errors

Nature serves as a good example of how trial and error can be used to make changes. Every now and then genetic mutations occur—errors in gene reproduction. Most of the time, these mutations have a deleterious effect on the species, and they drop out of the gene pool. But occasionally, a mutation provides the species with something beneficial, and that change will be passed on to future generations. The rich variety of all species is due to this trial and error process. If there had never been any mutations from the first amoeba, where would we be now?

Summary

There are places where errors are inappropriate, but the germinal phase of the creative process isn't one of them. Errors are a sign that you are diverging from the well-traveled path. If you're not failing every now and then, it's a sign you're not being very innovative.

☐ *TIP #21:* If you make an error, use it as a stepping stone to a new idea you might not have otherwise discovered.

☐ *TIP #22:* Differentiate between errors of "commission" and those of "omission." The latter can be more costly than the former. If you're not making many errors, you might ask yourself, "How many opportunities am I missing by not being more aggressive?"

☐ *TIP #23:* Strengthen your "risk muscle." Everyone has one, but you have to exercise it or else it will atrophy. Make it a point to take at least one risk every twenty-four hours.

☐ *TIP #24:* Remember these two benefits of failure. First, if you do fail, you learn what doesn't work; and second, the failure gives you an opportunity to try a new approach.

7. "Play Is Frivolous."

The Moment of Conception

Exercise: During what kinds of activities and situations do you get your ideas? For example, doing routine work, as a response to questions, during or after physical exercise, late at night, driving, in the company of others, etc.

I've asked this question of thousands of people. The answers I've received can be grouped into two categories. The first is "necessity," and it is represented by replies such as:

☞ "When I'm faced with a problem."

☞ "When things break down, and I have to fix them."

☞ "When there's a need to be filled."

☞ "When the deadline is near…that's the ulti-mate inspiration."

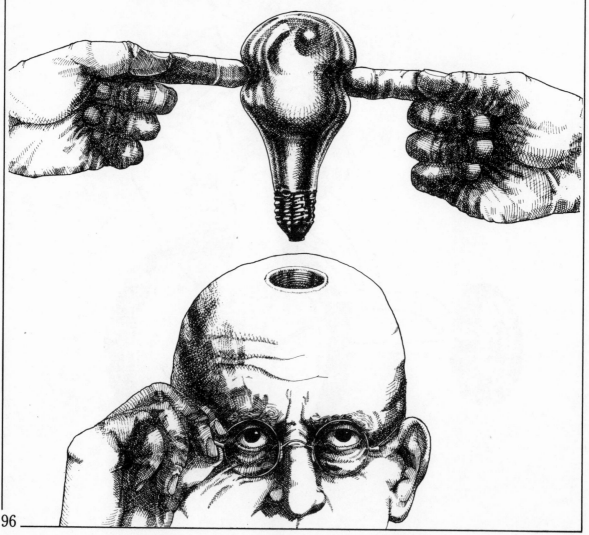

These responses bear out the old adage "necessity is the mother of invention." But interestingly enough, an equal if not greater number of people get their ideas in just the opposite situation, and they respond along these lines:

☞ "When I'm just playing around."

☞ "When I'm doing an unrelated activity."

☞ "When I'm toying with the problem."

☞ "When I'm not taking myself too seriously."

☞ "After my second beer."

From this I conclude that necessity may be the mother of invention, but play is certainly the *father.* As we said in the opening chapter, a playful attitude is fundamental to creative thinking. Indeed, I'll bet that you generate most of your new ideas when you are playing in your mental playground. That's because your defenses are down, your mental locks are loosened, and there is little concern with the rules, practicality, or being wrong.

Play And Learning

Most of life presents you with a win/lose proposition: if you don't win, you lose. This is true for most games and sporting events, elections, coin-tosses, bets, arguments, and the like. When you play, however, a different logic is at work: a win/no-win logic. This is an important difference because it means that instead of being penalized for our mistakes, we learn from them. Thus, when we win, we win, when we don't, we learn. This is a nice arrangement; the only thing play costs is the time to do it.

Children know that play is a good way to learn. Take a look at kids kicking a soccer ball. They'll pass it around, play all sorts of games with it, have fun with it, and most important, they will improve their soccer skills. Watch children play with a computer. They will experiment and try all kinds of approaches. Pretty soon, they are proficient. One reason children are so good at play is that they don't know all of the "supposed to's."

The ancient Greeks knew that learning comes from playing. Their concept for education (*paideia*) is almost identical to their concept for play (*paidia*). Perhaps, Plato was thinking this when he said, "What, then, is the right way of living? Life must be lived as play." If you are playing, then you are still learning and living.

Play And Work

Some people, however, think that if you're just playing at something, then you're really not working on it. Their attitude is, "Stop playing games and get down to business." They see work and play as two mutually exclusive boxes, and if you aren't producing hard tangible results, then you aren't working. They feel that *"play is frivolous."*

One of my clients, a computer architect, has this to say about the subject: "Play is what I do for a living; the work comes in organizing the results of the play." He realizes that there are two sides to the creative process. The play side enables him to try various approaches (perhaps some traditional ones, some fantastic ones, and some crazy ones), to learn what works and what doesn't and to take this knowledge to germinate new ideas. The work side enables him to take what he has learned, evaluate it, corroborate his findings with existing knowledge, and to put it into a form which will be useful.

Another client, a satellite design manager, told me that at one of his design meetings everyone was in a very playful mood. People started making fun of the satellite. They made jokes about it. They made bad puns about it. They even played with the whole notion of what a satellite is. The meeting turned out to be their most productive one in months. The next week, everyone approached their design problems in a serious mood, and no new ideas were generated.

A Fun Environment

One of play's products is fun—one of the most powerful motivators around. I've noticed that a fun working environment is much more productive than a routine environment. People who enjoy their work will come up with more ideas. The fun is contagious, and everybody works harder to get a piece of that fun.

One man, the president of a microprocessor company, told me that playfulness is one of his keys to success.

"When we hire new people, we're not so concerned with how intelligent or efficient they are. To us, the important characteristics are their playfulness and their intensity. When people have these two traits, they're enthusiastic— and these are the ones who generate new ideas." I might add that the word 'enthusiasm' comes from the Greek word _enthousiasmos_ which means 'the God within you.' Enthusiastic people seem to have access to a spirit which serves as the source of their inspiration.

Another client had this to say about the interrelationship of play and innovation: "Humor, frivolity, and play have a place in this world. Most large companies should remember that they began with a person enjoying himself in the garage. Too many of today's managers, however, have eliminated fun and humor from the job, and hence have eliminated creativity." To these people, I dedicate Laroff's credo:

It is not so important to be serious as it is to be serious about the important things.

The monkey wears an expression of seriousness which would do credit to any great scholar. But the monkey is serious because he itches.

The Moebius Stepping Stone

Some of the most important human inventions and ideas were originally conceived for the purpose of play—their practical value to be discovered later.

A good example of this is the Moebius strip, a one-sided surface which has many unexpected properties. This topological idea was discovered by the German mathematician and astronomer Augustus Ferdinand Moebius (1790–1868).

You can make a Moebius strip by taking a strip of paper and making a loop out of it. But before connecting the two ends, give one of them a half-twist. This loop now only has one side. You can prove this to yourself by taking a pencil and drawing a line all the way around the loop. Soon you will come back to your starting point. You will have covered the entire loop, thus proving that it has only one side. (It also has only one edge!)

Now take a pair of scissors and cut the strip along the line you have just drawn. What happens? Most loops, when cut in half, form two smaller loops. But this isn't the case with the Moebius strip—it becomes one loop twice as long (but now it has two sides and is no longer a Moebius strip).

Now try cutting a Moebius strip into thirds.

This produces another surprise: two intertwined loops, one a two-sided loop and the other a Moebius strip.

For years, the Moebius strip was considered to be the "plaything of topology"—a nice amusement but not much more. In the last forty years, however, some practical applications have been found for the Moebius strip. Rubber manufacturers have used the Moebius strip for conveyor belts. The belt lasts longer because both sides are actually one and receive equal wear. Electronic engineers have found that a resistor with a twist bent back upon itself performs its function more efficiently. A continuous loop in a cassette cartridge will play twice as long if it has a twist in it. Chemists are exploring ways of making molecules in the shape of the Moebius strip. When they split, they get bigger rather than smaller.

Flexibility of Thinking Problems

To end this chapter on play, it's only fitting to give you some problems to play with. Each problem is an equation which can be solved by substituting the appropriate words for the letters. Have fun with them!

Examples: 3F. = 1Y. (3 Feet = 1 Yard)

4L.C. = G.L. (4 Leaf Clover = Good Luck)

1. M. + M. + N.H. + V. + C. + R.I. = N.E.

2. "1B. in the H. = 2 in the B."

3. 8D. − 24H. = 1W.

4. 3P. = 6

5. H.H. & M.H. at 12 = N. or M.

6. 4J. + 4Q. + 4K. = All the F.C.

7. S. & M. & T. & W. & T. & F. & S. are D. of W.

8. A. + N. + A.F. + M.C. + C.G. = A.F.

9. T. = L.S. State

10. 23Y. − 3Y. = 2D.

11. E. − 8 = Z.

12. Y. + 2D. = T.

13. C. + 6D = N.Y.E.

14. Y. − S. − S. − A. = W.

15. A. & E. were in the G. of E.

16. My F.L. and South P. are both M.C.

17. "N.N. = G.N."

18. N. + P. + S.M. = S. of C.

19. 1 + 6Z. = 1M.

20. "R. = R. = R."

21. A.L. & J.G. & W.M. & J.K. were all A.

22. N. + V. + P. + A. + A. + C. + P. + I. = P. of S.

23. S. + H. of R. = U.S.C.

Summary

If necessity is the mother of invention, play is the father. Use it to fertilize your thinking.

☐ *TIP #25:* The next time you have a problem, play with it.

☐ *TIP #26:* If you don't have a problem, take the time to play anyway. You may find some new ideas.

☐ *TIP #27:* Make your work place a fun place to be.

8. "That's Not My Area."

The Solar Cell

A solar energy lab technician has a problem. Her research lab is experimenting with a new solar cell material, gallium arsenide, which is causing her difficulties in the slicing stage of cell production. Her task is to use a special high-speed wafer saw to make precision cuts in the material. But every time she cuts the material it cracks. She tries changing the position of her saw. The material still cracks. She is frustrated.

At home that weekend, she is in her husband's shop watching him make cabinets. She notices that when he wants to make precision cuts on certain types of wood, he *reduces* (rather than increases) the saw's cutting speed. She gets an idea: why not try the same approach on the gallium arsenide. She does, and it works.

What this woman did is an important part of creative thinking: recognizing the basic idea of one situation and applying it to another. The benefits of transferring knowledge gained in one area to another seem obvious. Why don't people do it more often?

One answer is specialization. As a strategy for managing information, specialization is essential. There is so much going on that it's impossible to pay attention to everything. Each second our nervous systems are bombarded by approximately 100,000 bits of information. If we responded to that much information, our nervous systems would snap. It would be like a clam trying to siphon up all the sludge in the San Francisco Bay—it just can't be done. Thus, one benefit of specialization is that it allows us to reduce the amount of irrelevant and trivial outside information we take in.

Similarly, as a strategy for getting along in the world, specialization is a necessity. In order to be effective in almost any endeavor—business, sports, academe, technology, cooking—you have to narrow your area and become an expert at it. Look at baseball. It used to be that relief pitchers were used sparingly; the starters were expected to go all the way. Now there is a whole array of specialized relievers: long relievers, intermediate relievers, short relievers, relievers who throw smoke to right-handed batters, etc. Look at the variety of different types of accountants: tax specialists, management services specialists, estate planning specialists, audit specialists, and so on. And the more complicated things become the higher the walls go. When I was in graduate school, I knew a marine biologist who was unable to talk with a molecular biologist because of the specialized nature of their disciplines. So we have a situation where people know more and more about less and less.

As a strategy for creative thinking, however, specialization can be dangerous because it can lead to the attitude. *"That's not my area."* When this happens, a person may not only delimit his problems to too small an area, he may also stop looking for ideas in other fields.

The Blue Capacitor

How many times have you heard someone say, "That's an engineering problem," "That's an accounting problem," or "That's a marketing problem"? We hear it all the time. Very few problems, however, are pure engineering problems; most are engineering and manufacturing problems —and perhaps even marketing problems. Most data processing problems are not only DP problems, but also communications and finance problems. But if a person thinks, "that's not my area," he probably won't be defining the problem in such broad terms.

Here is an example of some of the consequences of this attitude. One of my manufacturing clients had a single-sourced capacitor designed into a circuit-board his company was producing. People in manufacturing go out of their way to avoid "single-sourced" parts, i.e., those produced by only one outside vendor. They reason that if only one vendor is producing a particular sub-component, then an entire manufacturing group can be idled if anything happens to the vendor's capability to produce.

Things were fine until the vendor had production problems and could no longer meet demand. My client spent a lot of time attempting to track down more capacitors, but was unsuccessful. Finally, he went back through five layers of management to the design department to see how critical this capacitor was, and if it would be possible to use a replacement. When the design engineer was asked why this particular capacitor had been chosen, he replied, "I chose it because it's blue, and it looks good on the circuit board." The designer had never bothered to consider what impact such a choice would actually have on getting the product out the door. His tunnel-vision had prevented him from even looking for such a potential problem.

This happens in other professions as well. One of my brothers-in-law is a physician. He has told me that he has noticed a tendency on the part of some doctors to look at their patients from the point of view of their specialties. For example, the orthopedic surgeons with this attitude don't look at their patients as people, but as a set of bones; the cardiologists look at their patients as sick or healthy hearts, and so on. Thus, they overlook the role the mind plays in healing. As a reaction to this, we are seeing the rise of holistic medicine and the wellness movement.

Crossing the Boundaries

I have consulted for the movie and television industries, the advertising industry, high technology research groups, marketing groups, artificial intelligence groups, and art departments. The one common denominator I have found is each culture feels that it is the most creative, and that its members have a special elixir for new ideas. I think this is nice; *esprit de corps* helps to create a good working environment. But I also feel that television people could learn one heck of a lot from software people, and that R&D people could pick up a few ideas from advertising. Every culture, industry, discipline, department, and organization has its own way of dealing with problems, its own metaphors, models, and methodologies. But often the best ideas come from cutting across disciplinary boundaries and looking into other fields for new ideas and questions. Many significant advances in art, business, technology, and science have come about through a cross-fertilization of ideas. And to give a corollary, nothing will make a field stagnate more quickly than keeping out outside ideas.

Here are just a few examples of how people have taken ideas from one field and used them to make discoveries in another:

☞ An aerospace manager told me that several years ago he took up the hobby of designing and constructing backyard waterfalls for himself and his friends. "I don't know why," he said, "but designing waterfalls has made me a better manager. It has brought me a lot closer in touch with ideas such as 'flow,' 'movement,' and 'vibration' which are difficult to put into words, but which are important in the communication between two people."

☞ I read recently about a birth control device developed by a gynecologist collaborating with a dentist. An unusual combination! We'd expect the gynecologist; who else specializes in female anatomy? But the dentist? The dentist, however, makes much of his living working with forms, shapes, and molds. But usually this kind of knowledge is kept separate from gynecologists.

☞ The real estate entrepreneur Frank Morrow explains that he got his entrepreneurial education while attending the Graduate School of Business at Stanford—but not in the usual way. "I took all of the required courses in marketing, finance, accounting, and so on, but I learned more about business from a drawing course taught by the artist Nathan Olivera. What Olivera taught was: 'All art is a series of recoveries from the first line. The hardest thing to do is to put down the first line. But you must.' The same is true in business. You must act. A lot of business school types analyze things to death and never get around to acting. Perhaps more of them should take drawing courses."

Hunting Grounds

It's one thing to be open to new ideas; it's quite another to go on the offensive and actively hunt for them. I encourage you to be a "hunter" and search for ideas outside your area. This should be easy for you; you're already biologically equipped to be a hunter. For the past four million years our species has been evolving and developing, it has spent all except the last 20,000 years as hunters. This means that you have the eyesight, nervous system, and brain to be a hunter—to go looking for ideas and information in outside areas.

Exercise: Where do you hunt for ideas? What people, places, activities, and situations do you use to get new ideas?

I've asked many people this question. Here are some of their ideas.

Magic. Through the study and performance of magic, I've learned the power that certain symbols have when they are associated with one another. I've taken this knowledge and applied it to sales and product demonstrations.

Acting Class. From acting class I have been able to appreciate the impact that positive encouragement has on a person. I have seen some performances that were so bad I was embarrassed to watch. But the acting coach gave the person criticism in an encouraging way. As a result, these people were able to grow as actors. I think that there is a lesson here for many areas of life.

Family Trips. Whenever our family goes on vacation, I have made it a practice to take them on a tour through an operating plant to see how things are made and what procedures are used. We have seen sheet factories, record factories, distilleries, and ceramic factories.

Junk Yards. Going to a junk yard is a sobering experience. There you can see the ultimate destination of almost everything we desire.

Different People. I like to spend time with people whose value systems are different from my own. I like to see what's important to them, and that gives me a perspective on what's important to me.

Daydreaming to a Sound Effects Record. It really sets my mind free.

Flea Markets. Flea markets are one of the last outposts of free enterprise. If you want to know what a free economy is all about, go to a flea market. There you can see what values people place on things.

Old Science Magazines. I get ideas from reading old popular science magazines from the early twentieth century. There were many good ideas proposed then which couldn't be implemented because the materials weren't available then. However, the materials to implement them are available now.

History. History is filled with ideas. Napoleon marching on Moscow is really just project management. Mao carrying on a guerrilla war is like launching an advertising campaign.

Want Ads. The want ad section of the newspaper is what people are all about—not the front page. In the want ads you can see what people want, and that gives me ideas.

Sports. I think that sports provide a good source of ideas. I find an interesting parallel between why some teams always win and why some managers are able to motivate their people.

Studying a Subject on a Shallow Level. I get more ideas from a $2.98 basic introductory paperback than a $20 text. It's an example of the 20/80 rule in action.

Summary

Specialization is a fact of life. In order to function in the world, you have to narrow your focus and limit your field of view. When you're trying to generate new ideas, however, such information-handling attitudes can limit you. They not only may force you into delimiting your problems too narrowly, they may also prevent you from looking in outside areas for ideas.

To counteract the effects of specialization, we might heed the advice Edison gave to his colleagues: "Make it a habit to keep on the lookout for novel and interesting ideas that others have used successfully. Your idea has to be original only in its adaptation to the problem you are working on." Here are some tips that will help you improve your hunting ability:

☐ **_TIP #28:_** Develop the hunter's attitude, the outlook that wherever you go, there are ideas waiting to be discovered.

☐ **_TIP #29:_** Don't get so busy that you lose the free time necessary for idea-hunting. Schedule hunting time into your day and week. Little side excursions can lead to new hunting grounds.

☐ **_TIP #30:_** Develop different kinds of hunting grounds. The wider and more diversified your knowledge, the more places you will have to draw from.

☐ **_TIP #31:_** Look for analogous situations. Often problems similar to yours have been solved in other areas.

☐ **_TIP #32:_** When you "capture" an idea, be sure to write it down.

9. "Don't Be Foolish."

Scene #1

A man walks into the waiting room of a doctor's office. He looks around and is surprised by what he sees: everybody is sitting around in their underwear. People are drinking coffee in their underwear, smoking cigarettes in their underwear, reading magazines in their underwear, and carrying on conversations in their underwear. The man is shocked at first, but then decides that they must know something he doesn't. After about twenty seconds, he, too, takes off his clothes and sits down in his underwear to wait for the doctor.

Scene #2

A man waits patiently for an elevator in an office building. After a short period, the elevator arrives and the doors open. As he looks in, he notices that everybody is turned around and facing to the rear of the elevator. So, he, too, gets into the elevator and faces to the rear.

These scenes are from Allen Funt's 1960's television series *Candid Camera.* They both confirm what countless psychology tests have found, namely, the best way to get along is to go along.

All of us are subject to group pressures. If you study your own behavior, you will see how much you conform to various situations. Let's suppose that you are driving down the freeway, and everyone around you is going 65 miles per hour. (At this writing, the speed limit is still 55 MPH.) What happens? It is very difficult not to break the law; you get caught up in the "flow of traffic." Or, suppose that you are a pedestrian standing on the corner of an intersection in a major city. Ten or twelve other people are standing there with you. The sign says, "DON'T WALK," but no traffic is coming. Then one of the pedestrians crosses the street against the light. Soon another goes, and then another. In no time at all, all the other pedestrians have crossed the street against the light. And you do too, because you would feel really stupid being the only person still standing there.

Benefits of Conformity

Conformity serves at least two practical purposes. First, to live in society requires cooperation among its members. Without conformity, traffic would get tied up, production quotas would be missed, and the fabric of society would come apart. Part of the price we pay for the benefits of our social existence is a piece of our own individuality.

Second, in those situations in which we don't know our way around, what do we do? We look to others for the right way to act and the knowledge to get along. Suppose you are in a laundromat, and you are not quite sure how to operate the washing machine. What do you do? Probably look over to the person next to you and try the approach he is using.

The best example of this is St. Augustine. As a young priest in Milan, Italy, Augustine had a problem, and so he went to his bishop, Ambrose, for advice. It seemed that Augustine was going to spend the weekend in Rome. His problem was that in Rome it was customary to celebrate the Sabbath on Sunday, while in Milan the Sabbath was celebrated on Saturday. Augustine was confused as to which was the appropriate day. Ambrose solved Augustine's problem by telling him,

When in Rome, do as the Romans do.

Groupthink

New ideas, however, are not born in a conforming environment. Whenever people get together, there is the danger of "groupthink." This is the phenomenon in which group members are more interested in retaining the approval of other members rather than trying to come up with creative solutions to the problems at hand. Group pressure can inhibit originality and new ideas. Thus, when everyone thinks alike, no one is doing very much thinking.

Alfred Sloan knew the dangers of groupthink. In the late 1930's, Sloan was chairing a board meeting at General Motors. An idea was proposed and everyone present became very enthusiastic about it. One person said, "We'll make a lot of money with this proposal." Another said,

"Let's implement it as soon as possible." And still another said, "We'll knock the pants off our competition." After the discussion, Sloan said, "It's now time to vote on the proposal." The vote went around the table, and one by one, each board member voted "Aye." When the vote came back to Sloan, he said, "I, too, vote 'Aye' and that makes it unanimous. And for that reason, I am going to table the proposal until next month. I don't like what's happening to our thinking. We're getting locked into looking at this idea in just one way, and this is a dangerous way to make decisions. I want each of you to spend the next month studying the proposal from a different perspective." A month went by, and the proposal was brought up again at the next board meeting. This time, however, it was voted down. The board members had had an opportunity to break through the effects of groupthink.

The Fool

Any decision-maker and creative thinker (and we all are) has to deal with the problem of conformity and groupthink. But how? One idea is a device used by royalty in the Middle Ages and Renaissance to protect themselves from sycophantic counsellors: the fool.

The king's advisers were often yes-men—they told the king whatever he wanted to hear. The king knew that this wasn't a good way to make decisions. Therefore, it was the fool's job—indeed he had a license to do this—to parody any proposal under discussion. The fool's jokes whacked the king's thinking and forced him to examine his assumptions. In this way, the king protected himself from groupthink and generated new ideas.

How can we play the fool? There are many right ways to do it.

The fool might use a ridiculous form of logic. There was a fool who carried a live bomb in his briefcase whenever he flew. After a while, he was stopped by the authorities who asked him why he did it. "For my own safety," the fool replied. "One night, I calculated that the odds of someone carrying a bomb on an airplane were 1 in 10,000. That frightened me, and I decided that I would never fly again. Then I realized that the odds of there being two live bombs on a plane were 1 in 50,000,000. And ever since then, I've always taken mine with me."

The fool might deny that a problem exists at all and in doing so would reframe the situation. Most people think recessions are bad. Not the fool. He would say, "Recessions are good. Why? They make people work more efficiently. People work harder when they are insecure about the future of their jobs. Also, most companies have a fair amount of fat in them. Recessions force them to trim back to their fighting weight and be more aggressive."

The fool might be silly. There was the fool who was worried that if the world were a duck, there would be earthquacks.

The fool will try to reverse our standard assumptions. He might say, "If a man is sitting on a horse facing the rear, why do we assume that it is the man who is backwards and not the horse?"

The fool can be absurd. Having lost his donkey, the fool got down on his knees and began thanking God. A passerby saw him and asked, "Your donkey is missing; what are you thanking God for?" The fool replied, "I'm thanking Him for seeing to it that I wasn't riding the donkey at the time. Otherwise, I would be missing too."

The fool will extol the trivial and trifle the exalted. He will parody the rules. That's all part of his job. But in doing so, the fool stimulates our creative juices. Foolish ideas can jolt the mind in the same way that a splash of cold water wakes up a sleeping man. Thus, the fool forces us to think—even for just an instant—about what we think is real. Whatever assumptions we hold about the nature of things must suddenly be suspended, and the field of view greatly widened.

This is good. In a time when things are changing very quickly, who is to say what's right and what's foolish. As Einstein said,

A question that sometimes drives me hazy: am I or are the others crazy?

Sometimes the fool makes more sense than the wise man. Many of the most foolish ideas from five years ago are now a reality.

The Fools and the Rules

In my seminars, I provide an opportunity for people to practice playing the fool. We play a game called "The Fools and the Rules." It's easy to play; you take your holiest sacred cow and sacrifice it on the altar of foolishness. Here are some examples:

RULE: "Always be polite on the telephone."

FOOL: "Are you kidding? Abusive behavior cuts down on phone time. It also gives our public relations department more work. It would eliminate the hold button on the telephone as well as lead to honest employee relationships. Finally, rude telephone manners could serve as an outlet for employee stress."

RULE: "No smoking in the refinery." (This was from an oil company.).

FOOL: "That's silly. If we allowed smoking, we'd have fewer old-age benefits to pay out. It would also get rid of the lung diseases people have gotten by working in the refinery. It would cover up our pollution. It would force our tanks to be safer (no leaks) because of the possibility of explosion. And finally, it would enable us to re-build ala Germany and Japan to get up to current technology."

RULE: "Always communicate through the proper chain of command so as not to surprise your boss."

FOOL: "That's a waste of time. After all, bosses like surprises—they're fun! This would remove any chance for preconceptions (and we all know that preconceptions get in the way of creative ideas). This would also demonstrate how much goes on without anybody knowing. In addition you would be provided with a means of visibility because you'd always be called on to the carpet."

RULE: "Our company is 'Committed to Excellence.'"

FOOL: "How about just 'Committed'? Or maybe 'committed to incompetence.' Think of the possibilities! We'd have less development time, less quality control, lower training costs, and no backlogs. Also, part shortages wouldn't hold up production. Not only that, we would improve our chances of reaching our design goals. Also, we wouldn't be afraid to try new ideas—after all, what would we have to lose?

"Think of it from the customer's point of view: he would have a pleasant surprise whenever one of our products worked. He would have reduced expectations and wouldn't be disappointed as often.

"In the past we have been able to sell our products based on their technical merits. With mediocre products, however, we would have to learn how to sell. But that wouldn't be difficult. We'd also have a larger market. There are more mediocre people in the world than excellent ones. And, after all, nothing succeeds like mediocrity because everybody understands it so well."

As you can see, playing the fool is a lot of fun. It is also a great way to generate ideas and examine your assumptions. While the ideas produced may not be immediately useful, it may happen that a foolish idea will lead to a practical, creative idea. And if you come up empty, at least you'll understand why the rule was there in the first place.

Summary

Niels Bohr once said, "There are some things that are so serious you have to laugh at them." He makes a good point. Some people are so closely married to their ideas that they put them up on a pedestal. It's difficult, however, to be objective if you have a lot of ego tied up in your idea.

☐ *TIP #33:* Occasionally, let your "stupid monitor" down, play the fool, and see what crazy ideas you can come up with. Who knows, there may even be a job for you at the nearest royal domain.

☐ *TIP #34:* Recognize when you or others are conforming or putting down the fool. Otherwise, you may be setting up a "groupthink" situation.

☐ *TIP #35:* May the farce be with you.

10. "I'm Not Creative."

The Toilet Paper Shortage

"What concerns me is not the way things are, but rather the way people think things are."

—Epictetus

Several years ago, Johnny Carson made a joke on his television show that there was a toilet paper shortage in this country. He then went on to describe what some of the more dire consequences of this shortage might be. The implication of this joke was that the viewers had better go out and stock up on toilet paper right away or else they would have to face these consequences. The subject made for a good laugh, but there was in fact no toilet paper shortage at all. Within several days, however, a real shortage did develop. Because people thought there was a shortage, they went out and bought up all of the toilet paper they could find, and, as a result, they disrupted the normal flow of toilet paper distribution.

This serves as a good example of the self-fulfilling prophecy. This is the phenomenon whereby a person believes something to be true which is not, acts on that belief, and by his action causes the belief to become true. As you can see, the self-fulfilling prophecy is a case where the world of thought overlaps with the world of action. And it happens in all avenues of life.

Businessmen are quite familiar with self-fulfilling prophecies. In fact, the whole notion of business confidence is based on them. If a businessman thinks that the market is healthy (even though it may not be), he will invest money in it. This raises other people's confidence, and pretty soon the market will be healthy.

Educators are also aware of self-fulfilling prophecies. Several years ago, a teacher in New York was told that she had a class of gifted children, when in fact she had an ordinary class. As a result, she went out of her way to develop her students. She spent more time preparing her lessons and staying after class to give them ideas. The class, in turn, responded in a positive way, and scored higher than average on the same tests which had previously classified them as average. Because they were treated as gifted children, they performed as gifted children.

The same phenomenon is found in athletics. I've noticed that one of the chief differences between winners and losers in athletic competition is that the winners see themselves as winning and the losers generally give themselves a reason or an excuse to lose. A person who exemplifies this is Bob Hopper, a college swimming teammate of mine at Ohio State in the mid-1960's. Bob was an NCAA champion who rarely lost a race. One day at the pool, I asked him why he won all of his races. He responded:

> There are several reasons. First of all, my strokes are all well developed. Second, I work out hard—I always put in all of my yards. Third, I take good care of myself and eat right. But my top competitors generally do these three things as well. So the key difference between just "being good" and "winning" is my mental preparation before each meet.
>
> Starting each day before the meet, I run the following movie through my mind. I see myself coming into the Natatorium, with three thousand cheering fans sitting in the stand and the lights reflecting off of the water. I see myself going up to the starting block, and my competitors on each side. I hear the gun go off, and can see myself diving into the pool and taking the first stroke of butterfly. I can feel myself pulling through, taking another stroke, and then another. I see myself coming to the wall, turning, and pushing off into the backstroke with a small lead. The lead gets bigger with my underwater pull. Then I push off into the breast stroke. That's my best stroke and that's where I really open it up. And then I bring it home in the freestyle. I see myself winning!
>
> I run this movie through my mind thirty-five or forty times before each meet. When it finally comes time to swim, I just get in and win.

Bob seems to be telling us that just thinking a particular thought can have an enormous impact on the world of action.

Self-Esteem

Exercise: Are you creative? (Check the appropriate box.)

☐ YES   ☐ NO

Several years ago, a major oil company was concerned about the lack of creative productivity among some of its Research and Development personnel. To deal with this problem, top management brought in a team of psychologists to find out what differentiated the creative R&D people from the less creative ones. The hope was that their findings could be used to stimulate the less creative people.

The psychologists asked the scientists all kinds of questions ranging from what their educational background was to where they grew up to what their favorite color was. After three months of study, the psychologists found that the chief factor which separated the two groups was:

The creative people *thought* they were creative and the less creative people didn't think they were.

As a consequence, the people who thought they were creative allowed themselves to get into a germinal frame of mind and play with their knowledge. The "I'm not creative" people were either too practical or routinized in their thinking.

Some "I'm not creative" people stifle themselves because they think creativity belongs only to people like Beethoven, Einstein, and Shakespeare. To be sure, these are some of the superluminaries of the creative firmament, but by and large, these people didn't get their big ideas right out of the blue. On the contrary, most of their big ideas came from paying attention to their *intermediate-size* ideas, playing with them, and making them big ideas. The same thing holds for most intermediate-size ideas. These come from *small* ideas which their creators paid attention to, and gradually worked into bigger things.

Thus, one of the major factors which differentiates creative people from lesser creative people is that creative people pay attention to their small ideas. Even though they don't know where one of these will lead them, they know that a small idea could lead to a big breakthrough, and they believe that they are capable of making it happen.

The Two Frogs

Once upon a time, two frogs fell into a bucket of cream.

The first frog, seeing that there was no way to get any footing in the white liquid, accepted his fate and drowned.

The second frog didn't like that approach. He started thrashing around in the cream and doing whatever he could to stay afloat. After a while, all of his churning turned the cream into butter, and he was able to hop out.

Moral: If you think you can find the second right answer, you are more likely to do so.

If you want to be more creative, believe in the worth of your ideas, and have the persistence to continue building on them. With this attitude, you'll take a few more risks, and break the rules occasionally. You'll look for more than one right answer, hunt for ideas outside your area, tolerate ambiguity, look foolish every now and then, play a little bit, engage in "what-if" and other soft thinking approaches, and be motivated to go beyond the status quo. And finally, you will be able to whack yourself into doing all of these things.

Summary

The worlds of thought and action overlap. What you think has a way of becoming true.

☐ *TIP #36:* Whack yourself into trying new things and building on what you find—especially the small ideas. The creative person has the self-faith that these ideas will lead somewhere. Good Luck!

Whack, whack, whack!

Examination.

Here's an opportunity to take some ideas you've gotten from *A Whack on the Side of the Head* and carry them into action. Good luck!

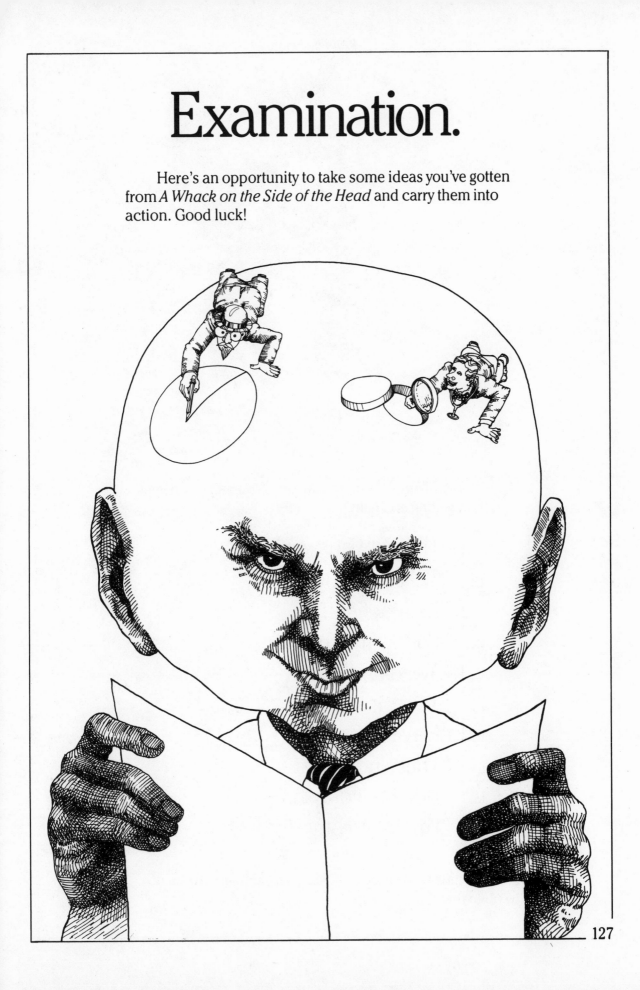

1.   Which (if any) of the mental locks sometimes prevent you from getting and using ideas.

☐   "The right answer."
☐   "That's not logical."
☐   "Be practical."
☐   "Follow the rules."
☐   "Avoid ambiguity."
☐   "To err is wrong."
☐   "Play is frivolous."
☐   "That's not my area."
☐   "Don't be foolish."
☐   "I'm not creative."

2.   For those locks you checked, what things can you do to open them?

3. What is your creative thinking style?

A) How would you rate yourself as a *magician*? How frequently do you ask "what-if" questions, or use impractical ideas as stepping stones to practical new ones?

1	2	3	4	5	6	7	8	9	10
Never		Seldom			Sometimes			Often	

B) How would you rate yourself as a *revolutionary?* How frequently do you question assumptions, challenge the rules, or discard obsolete ideas?

1	2	3	4	5	6	7	8	9	10
Never		Seldom			Sometimes			Often	

C) How would you rate yourself as a *poet*? How frequently do you use soft thinking tools such as the metaphor and ambiguity to generate ideas?

1	2	3	4	5	6	7	8	9	10
Never		Seldom			Sometimes			Often	

D) How would you rate yourself as a *hunter*? How frequently do you hunt for ideas in outside areas?

1	2	3	4	5	6	7	8	9	10
Never		Seldom			Sometimes			Often	

E) How would you rate yourself as a *fool*? How frequently do you break up potential "groupthink" situations?

1	2	3	4	5	6	7	8	9	10
Never		Seldom			Sometimes			Often	

4.   There is a saying that Frederick the Great (1712–1786) lost the battle of Jena (1806). This means that for twenty years after his death, the army perpetuated his successful organization instead of adapting to meet the change in the art of war.

What are some ideas and practices in your organization that have been successful in the past but which are limiting your productivity and growth now? How can you get rid of them?

5.   What if the job you have now ceased to exist tomorrow? What would you do? What are three alternatives?

6.   Think of three "what if" questions that pertain to a situation you are currently working on. Use these to stimulate ideas and expand your perspective into the possible.

7.   Think of one of your company's main products or services. What strange or zany uses can you think of for this product? How would you market this product in this new application?

8.   Think of two captions for this picture.

9.   Peter Drucker was once asked by a manager what skills he should learn in order to be a better manager. "Learn how to play the violin," Drucker told the man. What outside activity might you cultivate to make you more creative?

10.   Make a metaphor for a problem or project you are currently working on.

11.   Propose to your boss that you spend one or two days in the next month doing some unusual operation or activity outside your specialty. What would it be? What would make it worthwhile from his point of view, i.e. how would you sell him on the idea?

12.   What are the three biggest errors or failures you've had in the past three years? What were their beneficial consequences for you?

13.   List five things you can do to exercise your "risk muscle." What is the most you can lose by taking these risks? What will you gain?

14.   Suppose you have been sent to an oracle on behalf of your organization. You have been given two prophecies. The first pertains to the present, the second to the future. How would you interpret them?

   a. *Breakthrough.* One must resolutely make the matter known at the court of the king. It must be announced truthfully. Danger. It is necessary to notify one's own city. It does not further to resort to arms. It furthers one to undertake something.

   b. *Enthusiasm.* It furthers one to install helpers and to set armies marching.

15.   How do you whack your thinking?

16.   What are you going to be doing one year from today? What creative things will you have accomplished? What goals will you have reached? What factors will have made it difficult to reach these goals?

A Final Whack.

The man in the stuffed chair is about to have an idea. What that idea is will depend on what thoughts are available to him, and that, of course, is directly related to his experience as a thinker. He could have a small idea, or he might even have a big idea.

Remember: There are a lot of good thinkers who sit around in stuffed chairs.

Now you can see that what started out as a simple story is beginning to develop a complex structure of its own. Indeed, you might even find yourself about to have an idea!

As we look closer, we can see that the man in the stuffed chair is forming a facial expression that hints he may have an idea.

Remember: Your facial expressions can give you away. Now, you as an observer may be still having an idea of your own. And maybe your idea is better than the man in the stuffed chair's idea.

Moral: If you have an idea, get out of your stuffed chair and put it into action. After all, someone else may have the idea first, and if he does...

THE NEXT ONE'S FOR YOU!

About The Author

(The First Right Answer.)

Roger von Oech is the founder and president of Creative Think, a Menlo Park, California based company specializing in innovation and creativity in business. Creative Think provides consulting, seminars, conferences, publications, and serves as an idea agency to innovators and entrepreneurs.

Prior to starting Creative Think in 1976, Roger was employed by IBM in the areas of data base and data communications. In addition, he has worked for Remington Rand in Amsterdam, The Netherlands.

Dr. von Oech is a Phi Beta Kappa graduate from the Ohio State University where he received both the President's Scholarship Award and the Scholar-Athlete Award. He earned his doctorate from Stanford University in a self-conceived interdisciplinary program in the History of Ideas.

He is married to Wendy (who also works for Creative Think), and they have a daughter, Athena.

About The Author

(The Second Right Answer.)

Sometimes I think the human mind is like a compost pile. It contains a variety of ingredients all stewing together toward the ultimate end of producing something useful. Some ingredients aid the process, some hinder it, and others are inert.

Many of the ideas in my own compost heap have come from my work as a creative thinking consultant in industry. I picked up the other ingredients from a variety of experiences. My sixth grade teacher, Mr. Rodefer, taught me that being creative and being obnoxious are sometimes very similar, but they are *not* the same thing. He taught me how to differentiate the two by giving me a creative license. We had an agreement: I'd run a lap around the school yard for every obnoxious act, and he would reward me for my new ideas. I learned to take chances. In addition to running 128 laps that year, I did some very creative things.

Some of my ideas came from hitchhiking around the country—I put about 30,000 miles on my right thumb in a five year period. I remember one ride in particular in which I learned about the economics of supply and demand. The driver was a Montana cowboy who was bootlegging pornography from San Francisco to Utah. He had discovered that there were people in the hinterlands who would pay three times the cover price for his four-color commodity.

I learned about competition from swimming. I remember one sweet summer when Paul McCormick and I spent successive weeks beating each other's time in the 100 free. The competition made us both faster.

As an undergraduate at Ohio State, I learned that someone from the corn belt could develop an appreciation for a culture twenty-five centuries long gone. In particular, I discovered the pre-Socratic philosopher Heraclitus who taught me that ambiguity can be a good thing when you're trying to generate new ideas.

Living in Germany taught me that you don't have to be a Marxist to believe that some changes should be made in the world.

I wrote my doctoral dissertation on the twentieth century German philosopher Ernst Cassirer, the last man to know everything. From him, I learned that it's a good thing to be a generalist; looking at the Big Picture helps to keep you flexible.

Working for IBM taught me that there are a lot of hardworking, highly-talented, narrowly-focused people in the business world.

In starting my own business, I discovered that you can have the greatest idea in the world, but if you can't sell it to other people, you're not going anywhere.

And in doing my work, I've learned that people enjoy having their minds stimulated, and that a whack on the side of the head can be a positive experience.

Recommended Reading

Edwin Abbott, *Flatland.* New York, Dover, 1953.

Ralph Caplan, *Notes On Connection.* Zeeland, Michigan: Herman Miller, 1978.

Fritjof Capra, *The Tao of Physics.* New York: Bantam, 1977.

Ernst Cassirer, *An Essay On Man.* New Haven: Yale University Press, 1944.

Arthur C. Clarke, *Childhood's End.* New York: Ballantine, 1953.

Edward de Bono, *New Think.* New York: Avon, 1971.

T.S. Eliot, *Four Quartets.* New York: Harcourt, Brace & World, 1943.

Euripides, *The Bacchae.*

Martin Gardner, *The Ambidextrous Universe.* New York: Mentor, 1969.

Willis Harman, *An Incomplete Guide to the Future.* Stanford: Stanford Alumni, 1975.

Walter Herdeg, editor, *The Graphis Annual.* Zurich: Graphis Press, annually.

Herman Hesse, *Narcissus And Goldmund.* New York: Noonday, 1969.

Douglas Hofstadter, *Gödel, Escher, Bach.* New York: Basic, 1979.

Homer, *The Odyssey.* Translated by Richmond Lattimore. New York: Harper & Row, 1965.

I Ching. Translated by Richard Wilhelm. Princeton: Princeton University Press, 1950.

Julian Jaynes, *The Origin of Consciousness in the Breakdown of the Bicameral Mind.* Boston: Houghton Mifflin, 1976.

Carl Jung, *Memories, Dreams, and Reflections.* New York: Random House, 1961.

Orrin E. Klapp, *Opening And Closing.* Cambridge: Cambridge University Press, 1978.

B. Kliban, *Never Eat Anything Bigger Than Your Head.* New York: Workman, 1976.

Arthur Koestler, *The Act Of Creation.* New York: Macmillan, 1964.

George Leonard, *The Silent Pulse.* New York: E.P. Dutton, 1978.

Pamela McCorduck, *Machines Who Think.* San Francisco: W.H. Freeman, 1979.

Robert McKim, *Experiences In Visual Thinking.* Monterey: Brooks/Cole, 1972.

William McNeil, *The Rise of the West.* Chicago: University of Chicago Press, 1963.

David Ogilvy, *Confessions of an Advertising Man,* New York: Ballantine, 1971.

Robert Pirsig, *Zen and the Art of Motorcycle Maintenance.* New York: Bantam, 1974.

Neil Postman, *Crazy Talk, Stupid Talk.* New York: Delta, 1976.

The Random House Encyclopedia. New York: Random House, 1977.

Antoine de Saint Exupery, *The Little Prince.* New York: Harcourt, Brace & World, 1943.

William Shakespeare. *King Lear.*

Peter S. Stevens, *Patterns In Nature.* Boston: Atlantic-Little, Brown, 1974.

Wendy von Oech, *First Birth.* Menlo Park: Creative Think, 1982.

James Watson, *The Double Helix.* New York: Signet, 1969.

Lynn White, *Dynamo and Virgin Reconsidered.* Cambridge, Mass.: MIT Press, 1968.

P.R. Whitfield, *Creativity In Industry.* Baltimore: Penguin, 1975.

Alexander Woodcock & Monte Davis, *Catastrophe Theory.* New York: Avon, 1980.

Index of Proper Names

I hope you enjoyed this book. If you have any thoughts or comments or creative experiences you would like to share, I would be delighted to hear from you. Address all correspondence to Creative Think, P.O. Box 7354, Menlo Park, California, 94025.

R.v.O.

How To Unlock Your Mind
For Innovation

A Whack
On The Side Of The Head